"ORPHANS" With Parents

Lifes struggles

M A R I A N   S T O V E R

authorHOUSE®

AuthorHouse™
1663 Liberty Drive
Bloomington, IN 47403
www.authorhouse.com
Phone: 1-800-839-8640

Published by AuthorHouse 5/11/2012

ISBN: 978-1-4685-7529-3 (e)
ISBN: 978-1-4685-7530-9 (sc)

Library of Congress Control Number: 2012906216

This Book is Dedicated to
My Grandaughter
Melissa Ann NOBLE

Everyone has a story to tell
and this is mine
I have found life to be very
tough at times
but very interesting
with prayer and the love
of my family and friends, I will
continue to enjoy my life.

Acknowledgments

I would like to give thanks to all the wonderful people who stood behind me and encouraged me to put my story down on paper.

To my good friend and mentor, Emily Feistritzer who is an accomplished writer and has published several of her own books, I thank you for all of your support and encouragement in spurring me on to fulfilling my dream of writing my story. You gave me the confidence and motivation I needed to move forward.

To my lovely niece, Maria Jackson who is a commercial artist, I thank you for offering your wonderful talents in helping me to illustrate the cover of my book. (Maria and her husband Tom are the wonderful parents to three delightful little boys.)

And to my lovely niece, Lisa Beckelheimer, who is an English professor, I thank you for using your talents in reviewing my book. (Lisa and her husband Tim are raising two handsome teenage boys.)

To my friend Liz, I thank you for providing me with positive feedback and constantly encouraging me to keep moving forward, and also to my granddaughter Mary.

To my youngest granddaughter Michelle, I thank you for saying "Grandma, hurry up and finish your book, I want to read it."

And finally to my lovely daughter Dorothy I want to thank you for all your help in working with me to finalize the content of my book. We laughed and cried as we read through some of the stories in the book. We also had some frustrating moments during the long and tedious process. You were very helpful to me as we patiently proceeded to fulfill my dream of telling my story. I love you, and I appreciate your patience.

Last, but certainly not least, I thank the Lord for all he has ever given me.

Chapter 1

It was in the year of 1935 that our parents, Rita and William Crawford, decided to go to Nova Scotia along with our grandma Crawford and my sister Joan. Joan was an infant at the time, and they were going to Nova Scotia to look for jobs. They hitched a ride whenever they could along the way. Our Grandma had left her husband. Later he did come after her and tried to get her to go back with him to Kentucky. On the way to Nova Scotia they happened to find jobs in Keene, New Hampshire, where they decided to stay and work. The following year my brother Floyd was born in July and I was born in November of 1937. Our paternal grandmother was very good to us and I was very fond of her.

I don't remember much about Keene, but I do remember the time when I was sitting in a wagon and deer came up and startled me and then just walked away slowly. Our mom used to tell stories of how I would strip down to nothing and go out in the snow and that she had a terrible time keeping clothes on me. She also told me that I fell and hit my chin on the table and almost bit my tongue in half. They said it was hanging by threads and they thought I would never talk again, but I did and now I tend to talk too much. I do remember that it was beautiful in Keene, and wasn't far from the ocean. This is what I remember most of my first home.

It was in April of 1939 that my brother Harry was born. Pacifiers did not exist back then but they would make us what they called a "sugar tit." They would take a rag and put sugar in it and tie it with a string and we would suck on it. I remember I called mine a "booie" and I would sometimes take Harry's "booie" away from him.

In 1939, my paternal grandmother was killed at the age of forty-four. It was said she fell out of a car going around a sharp curve in Keene. Most of our family believed her husband had pushed her out of the car during an argument. I remember everyone was very sad and crying, and I missed my grandma.

Shortly after our Grandma Crawford was killed, our mom's parents, the Gausepohls, came all the way to New Hampshire from Northern Kentucky to visit us along with our mom's younger sister, Aunt Edith. Aunt Edith was fourteen at the time. We were very young but we were very excited to meet them. They had never met my brothers and me because we were born in New Hampshire.

My Aunt, our mom, grandma and grandpa, my two brothers, my sister and I in New Hampshire in 1939.

My two brothers, myself and my big sister.

Our mom and dad in New hampshire.

Our grandma and grandpa.

Right after our grandparents visit our parents decided to leave New Hampshire and go back to Kentucky. Our parents lived in a flood prone area and knew a flood was coming because it had been raining off and on for weeks. They packed up the car and got us kids ready to go. As they drove off, we watched the house as it was being invaded by the floodwaters. Right before we drove off I remember our father took our box of pet, white mice and put them under the wheel of the car so they would die. We were all upset and crying.

When we got back to Kentucky, we lived in the country in an area called Sandford Town. Eventually the authorities kicked us out of that house, saying the building was condemned. There was no heat, no stove to cook food, no water or electricity, and it was wintertime.

Our maternal grandpa built our family a large square-frame house in Latonia Lakes. It was up to our dad to add walls and make it a home with several rooms, but that never happened because our dad was too lazy. Eventually we lost that place too.

Then we moved to the city in Northern Kentucky, across the river from Cincinnati. The next house we lived in was on Crescent Avenue and it overlooked the river. I remember that our mom used to polish our little white shoes and set them in the sun to dry on the front porch of the house. I liked those little white shoes.

Back in Kentucky with our Mom, my
sister and I and my two brothers.

Another house we lived in was on what everyone called the "fill". It was near the garbage dump at the bottom of a very steep hill. There was a huge field across the road where we played ball that was always flooded out. On one corner of the field there were some big concrete pipes that were bigger than we were tall. We always played in these pipes. Above the field was Dixie Highway. Dixie Highway had a sharp bend and big trucks would turn over if they were going too fast, and they would spill their loads. Our dad was always running across the ball field and up the hill to see what they had spilled. He would always bring stuff back. One time I remember they had spilled a lot of thread and sewing materials. Our dad snatched up all he could handle and brought it back home to us.

This house had three rooms. Our parents' bedroom had a full-size bed in it and a rollaway that some of us kids slept in. That was the same bed we were playing in one day when my brother Floyd got hurt. I remember Floyd was under the bed and we were jumping on it. He must have had his legs up against the springs as we were jumping, and he suddenly started screaming in pain. We had broken his leg. We felt awful and we didn't know what to do. Our parents weren't home and we were scared because he was in so much pain. After we found our parents they took him to the hospital.

Besides the beds in our parents' bedroom there were two dressers and a table with a lamp on it. In the living room, which was the middle room, there was a pot-bellied stove. We would build a fire in it to heat the house. Our mom would always stand in front of the pot-bellied stove with her dress pulled up and her hands on her hips with no underwear on. (She probably couldn't afford any.) There was a closet, one side-table, and a couple of boxes filled with clothes. There was never enough room for the clothes in the dressers. Some of us slept on these boxes of clothes because we didn't have enough beds. By this time there were four of us, and our mom was pregnant with her fifth child.

In the kitchen, there was a big black iron stove; we had to build a fire in it just to cook our breakfast and other meals. There was a table and some chairs and something they called a pantry cupboard. We didn't have a bathroom at first. Not too long after we moved in, Grandpa came and he put a bathroom in for us along with a tub, toilet, and sink. Our dad even helped him, which was surprising because our dad never did anything. We thought we were rich. Our wringer washing machine fit in there too, and we could help with the laundry right in the bathroom.

In July of 1940, my sister Beverly was born and in August of 1941 my sister Shirley was born. My brother Frank, whom we nicknamed "Butch", was born in January of 1944. Our mom always put the babies in a dresser drawer—I guess she never had a baby bed for the babies. We soon found out that our new baby brother Butch was allergic to regular milk but could actually drink goat's milk. We were lucky that our neighbor had some goats, and he was glad to give us the goat's milk for Butch to drink. I remember stretching a strange-looking nipple over a soft-drink bottle to be able to feed my brother this goat's milk. He thrived on it. When Butch was about eighteen months old we were all looking out the back bedroom door watching a furious storm roll by. Butch was always very curious and naturally he got too close to the door and he fell out. He landed right on a rock and put a nice little hole in the middle of his forehead. It seemed to bleed forever. My parents had him on a table and were trying to clean it up and he wanted no part of it. Every time they would put a bandage on it, he would rip it off, screaming his head off the whole time. He was quite a little stinker. Of course, we all blamed it on to the goat's milk that he had to drink as an infant. He was a really feisty little toddler.

My maternal grandparents were wonderful people and they were very helpful. A lot of families had a difficult time back then because of the depression. We did have two great aunts that seemed to be well off. They would help our mom sometimes. Our Aunts, Uncles and grandparents got tired setting us up each time we moved to a different house mostly because our parents would leave some of the furniture behind that they had already given to us and because our mom and dad would not help themselves. They just kept having more and more kids, wouldn't get jobs and spent lots of time at the bars.

I remember when my brother Harry was four years old and he had he wrecked his bicycle. His was seriously injured and he was screaming in pain. I was surprised when our dad actually carried him all the way to the hospital, which was about two miles away. I thought this was one time our dad acted like a dad. Soon after that, Joan also had a bad bicycle wreck and had to go to the hospital. She didn't break anything, but her leg was gouged really deep, and it scarred up pretty bad. Those scars never did go away.

We were left at home alone most of the time, even with the little ones and we didn't have much food. We were always hungry. Sometimes we would go and sit in our neighbors' garden and eat his tomatoes, potatoes and cucumbers. He was a good neighbor and understood. We also got food from the dumps, scraping out the mayonnaise jars, peanut-butter jars, and jelly jars, and eating stale and moldy bread. We even got our toys at the dump.

We would also go to the bar a lot where our parents would socialize. We would be sat at a table and told to be good. Some of the men in the bar would give us a nickel to buy a candy bar. Sometimes we were given pickled pigs feet to eat. They looked gross but they were pretty good to eat.

I remember one time our neighbor gave our mom a chicken and we watched while she wrung its neck and then stuck it in boiling water to pluck the feathers off and then she cooked it for dinner.

Once in a while, when our grandparents would visit, they would give us some pennies and we would be allowed to go to what we called the "jingle-bell store." We called it that because when you opened the door, the bell over the door would ring.

Sometimes when we would be walking home, we would find money on the road.

Our dad taught us to always keep our eyes down to the ground because he would say, "You never know what you might find." When we would find some money, he would say that he probably dropped it and then we would have to give it to him.

When we lived on the fill, we were flooded out just about every spring. Once when our dad was moving us out of the house that was surrounded by the floodwaters, he fell out of the boat. We thought it was funny, and he yelled at us for laughing at him. When the house got flooded out we had to stay at the Salvation Army. They would put us up until the floodwaters went down. While we were there we would go to the movies and we all got popcorn. My brother Harry would always save his popcorn for later. Once during the night, someone stole his popcorn. He cried and cried for a really long time. He was so upset, and he wanted to go home. He didn't care that the house was flooded out; he just wanted to go home. He eventually cried himself to sleep.

When Shirley was about two years old, our mom was using the old wringer-type washing machine and some of us kids were playing around and trying to help. Some how Shirley got her arm caught in the wringer. We couldn't figure how that happened because the wringer had to be cranked by hand. It tore her skin up and she still has a really bad scar on her arm that looks like a burn.

One summer when Shirley was just three years old a few boys from the neighborhood kidnapped her and took her to the woods and left her there. We were all frantic when we couldn't find her. She was later found tied to a tree. She wasn't hurt but she was very frightened.

Later that summer, my brother Floyd got a puppy. He wanted one really bad, so our dad got him one and they named him Duke. He was a really playful puppy but he had a bad habit of barking at cars. There weren't that many cars back then, but our yard was real close to the road. Duke could hear them coming blocks away, and he would start barking. One day a car purposely came into our small yard and ran over the little puppy. Floyd was really hurt, and he seemed to cry forever over Duke. It was just as well; we could not feed the dog properly anyway.

Because our family was poor we received rations from the government, called *commodities* that helped to keep us fed. The commodities included flour, sugar, powdered milk, powdered eggs, lard and a few other things that I can't recall. It was just the basics that you could make biscuits and gravy and bread with. It gave us some solid food for us to eat if our mom was there to fix it for us. It was very hard to feed nine people with the commodities that we got. If our dad had worked steadily, or even at all it would have been much better for the family. We wouldn't have had to depend on everyone else to help support our family. Our grandparents were great, but they could only do so much. After all, they had five other children, and I am sure some of them needed help once in a while too. I know they did the best they could. They loved us, and that was what was important.

One time our mom sent Floyd and me to the store for a jar of apple butter and a loaf of bread. On the way home from the store, we dropped the jar of apple butter, shattering it to pieces. We were scared to death to go home without it, so we played around for a while, trying to kill time. We did not want to go home and tell our mom that we dropped the jar of apple butter. She had given us all of the money she could find in the house. We both got yelled at and then spanked for being so careless. At least we had the bread, and we ate the usual: bread with lard spread on it and sugar sprinkled on top of the lard. We liked it, but apple butter would have been so much more of a treat for us.

Often we would have to go to the icehouse with the wagon and get a block of ice to put in the icebox to keep the milk and butter cold. There were always babies in the house that needed the milk. It was a long way to the icehouse, which was close to our grandma's house. It was about eight blocks from our house and very near to where we went to school. That was always a fun thing to do, and the men at the icehouse were really nice to us. We would have to hurry home, especially in the summertime, so the ice wouldn't start to melt too much. If the ice had water on top when we got home, we would be in trouble for not hurrying up more than we did. But we were strong, determined little kids and we didn't care if we got in trouble.

Going to school in winter was very difficult. We hardly ever had shoes to fit our feet. If we did find some shoes, they usually had holes in them. We would wear anything just to have something on our feet. It was awful when it was rainy or snowy and our feet would get wet. It was at least five blocks to school. We always looked like ragpickers because we were not taken care of very well. Even some of our own relatives did not want to be around us. I think they were ashamed of us because we looked so awful.

Several times we had to take our younger siblings to school with us if our mom was sick or having another baby. The teachers did not seem to mind; they would just give them some crayons and paper and let them do their own thing. They were very good. There would have been no one at home to care for them because our dad wouldn't take care of the little ones. He had his own life and didn't have time to care for us kids. After school we would take the younger kids back home with us and care for them ourselves.

Everyone once in a while a priest from our church would come by and talk to our mom to see how they could help us kids. One time they took all of us to the store and bought us all new shoes. We thought we were in heaven.

Our dad was pretty mean to us. He would slap us and kick us around and even got the belt out that he sharpened his razors with. One time when I was standing on a stool washing dishes, he came over and said they were not clean enough and kicked me right in the back. I fell down and doubled over and started to cry. He just picked me up and made me finish the dishes. I was only five at the time. He should have been doing the dishes himself, but he was too lazy.

It was Christmas of 1944, and for some reason the house was nice and clean when we came home from school. We never knew who came and cleaned it up so nice. We figured someone must have come by and helped our mom. We saw that there was a new rollaway bed for us kids, and also a baby bed for the baby. The rollaway was set up in the living room, and there was a nice Christmas tree, too. Later that evening, we were all curled up in the rollaway bed and we kept hearing bells outside. We were awfully excited. Our mom tried to quiet us down and she went to see who was outside the door. It was Santa Claus. He brought us lots of presents, of clothes and toys, and lots of candy, apples, oranges, and nuts. We were very happy little kids. Our parents went to bed and let us stay up to celebrate, and in the morning when we woke up the place was a mess. We had peanut shells and orange peels all over the place. We had to clean it all up, but we didn't care because we had lots of fun and lots of good food to eat for a change. We also had some new clothes and toys. I suspect our grandma and aunts had a hand in it, along with the Salvation Army and our church. It was the best Christmas we ever had by far. We always got a present from our godparents and Grandma and Grandpa but never anything like this from anyone else.

In March of 1945 when our mom was twenty-five years old she gave birth to her eighth child, on St. Patrick's Day. Of course she was named Patricia since she was born on St. Patrick's Day. While our mom was still in the hospital our dad came home from the bar and brought another man home with him. They were both very drunk. Later that night the man grabbed my sister Joan and started pawing all over her and hurting our sister, who was only ten years old at the time. Our dad was sound asleep in the chair in a drunken stupor right in front of them. Nothing fazed him, he couldn't even wake up to save his own daughter, or maybe he didn't want to. Who knows? My brothers and sisters and I didn't understand that he was molesting our sister. Joan was screaming and we were hiding in a closet, crying and screaming right along with her. The closet never had a door on it, so we could still see everything. We were petrified, and we did not know what to do. We just huddled together and cried. When the man left, we just stayed there and cried together until we just fell asleep.

A few months later, Floyd and I were getting ready for our First Communion and First Confession at our parish church where we went to school. I remember practicing for my First Confession with Sister Jana. She would take us one at a time into the cloakroom and talked to us about how we would tell the priest our sins and what else we had to do and say. The whole time she talked to me, she kept smoothing down the wrinkles in my dress and I was embarrassed. Our clothes were always so messy when we went to school but this was the first time I really remember feeling terrible about how my clothes looked. I was just seven years old.

When it was finally time to make my First Confession, I don't know what I said, but the next thing I knew the priest was telling me to come over to him in his cubicle. He sat me on his lap and talked to me from there. I was really scared, but he was very nice to me. After the way our dad treated us, I was scared to death of men. But to me, priests were different, they were from God, and I thought that meant they were okay.

Later I remember our grandma coming to our house to fit me for my First Communion dress that she was making for me. I had to try it on several times for her, and it was nice when she came to our house. She came over the morning of May 5th, our First Communion day, and stood me on the table to make sure my dress was just right. She fixed my hair, which was nothing but frizz because our mom had given me a permanent. Everyone else thought it was perfect, so it was okay with me. Our grandma also helped Mom get Floyd looking just right in his little white suit, and he looked more handsome than ever. He was a very sweet little boy. Everyone called him a "towhead" because of his light blond hair.

My brother and I on our first communion day, May 5th, 1945

After the ceremony, we went out with Grandma and Grandpa to have breakfast at the Anchor Grill restaurant near the church. Everyone liked going there, and it was only a block away from our Grandma's house. It was our favorite place to eat. Everyone was very friendly there. In the afternoon, we had to go back to the church to get enrolled in the scapular. The scapular was a dedication to the Blessed Mother. After that, we went to Grandma and Grandpa's house, where they had a party for us with all our cousins, aunts, uncles and a few friends of the family. One of my grandpa's cousins was a religious Brother. Since he wasn't actually a priest, he couldn't say Mass. I don't remember which order he was in but I knew it was in Ohio. I do remember he wore a Sacred Heart emblem on his cassock, and to me, he represented Jesus. I thought it was neat that he was there on our special day. It was one of the best days of my life because I received Jesus in Holy Communion and learned I could to talk to him.

A few weeks later a rat bit our baby sister Patty while she was sleeping in her bed. We had a dirt basement full of rats and we used to name them. We thought they were our pets and we wanted to play with them. It turns out that the rat was poisonous. Patty got rat-bite poisoning from the bite and had to spend a lot of time in the hospital. They thought she was going to die.

It was shortly after that that our parish priest came to visit our mom and dad again. I wondered if he was coming to visit more often because of what I had told the priest in my First Confession about what had happened to our sister Joan. I always thought it was my fault; because I was the bad guy who snitched, and thought I was going to get in trouble for it. Of course, the priest came to talk to our parents, but we were happy to see him because he had always been good to us. He always had a treat for us, whether it was food or candy. We didn't care; we just thought he came to help our mom after what had happened to Patty. The priest said he would be back the next day to take us for a nice long ride. Our mom was crying and we thought she was crying because of Patty being so sick.

I had already heard conversations from our aunts and uncles that they wanted to help our mom out by taking some of us kids. Each one of them would take their godchild. Grandma and Grandpa were going to care for Joan and Floyd and I was going to go live with my Aunt Marian. Aunt Erma and Uncle Harry wanted Harry to come live with them and Beverly was going to live with Aunt Dorothy. Aunt Alma was going to take in Shirley and Aunt Edith would care for Butch (Frankie). The baby was going to stay with our mom. But our mom wouldn't hear of it. I never understood why, she just said that she wanted us all to stay together. (That was a joke, we were not together.)

All seven of us before going to the orphanage, 1945

Well, the priest did come the next day, and he piled all seven of us into his car and took us on a nice long ride. He gave us candy to keep us busy on the way. It was the longest ride ever. We passed a lot of great big buildings and saw lots of pretty sights. Finally we came to a place right next to a church. He parked the car in a great big play-yard. There were a lot of children playing in the yard and they were all boys. There were swings and merry-go-rounds and boys riding bicycles. He told us to go play while he went inside to talk to someone. We were playing in the yard with the other children, having a great time, when we heard the bells ringing and all the children started to line up. Suddenly we realized that the priest had left, and he left us there. We thought he had forgotten us. We were scared, and we all held on to each other. Soon one of the sisters (nuns) in charge came and told us it was time to go and have some supper. She took us girls by the hand and told our brothers to go with another sister who came out to get them. We had no choice; we had to go with her because the priest had just left us behind. We went with the sister to a dining room where there were a lot of girls. The bigger girls helped us and told us where to sit and what to do. That was the very best meal we'd had in a long time—we couldn't get enough, but we still wanted someone to come and get us and take us home. We didn't want to stay but we had no choice, we had to obey the sisters. When we were finished eating, we were taken outside to play for a while. After that we were then taken into a great big room with lots of beds on each side of the room. They showed us which bed we would sleep in, and there was a "big" girl to look after each one of us and show us what to do. I was seven years old and my younger sisters were four and five years old. Our older sister Joan was ten years old and she was shown where the "big girls" would sleep. Since we were "little girls", we needed to be looked after. That first night, they kept us all together. After that, Joan was told she had to stay in the big girls' room. I thought it was because of what had happened to her at home. Soon they called all the rest of the children in and told us it was bedtime. They fine-combed our hair in case we had lice and put some smelly stuff on it. They gave us a bath, and cleaned us up real nice. They gave us some nice pajamas to sleep in, and we got ready for bed. It was all real nice, but we wanted to go home and we wanted our brothers to be with us, because we loved our brothers too. The nuns told us that we were going to stay there and that was to be our new home, and there was no one coming to get us so we had to stay. We all huddled together and cried so long that the nuns let us sit on the fire-escape steps so we wouldn't disturb the other children. We sat on those steps and cried, promising each other we would figure a way to get out of there and get our brothers and go home to our parents. We just cried until we all fell asleep. When we woke up in the morning, we were all in our beds.

This was our new home. Like it or not, we were stuck in an orphanage. We had two parents when most of the kids in there only had one parent or no parents at all.

Chapter 2

O n our first full day at the orphanage, the nuns took my two younger sisters, Beverly and Shirley, along with my baby brother Butch (Frankie) to what they called the "baby house." The nuns told us we had to call Butch by his given name Frankie. I was happy the younger kids were at least all together for now and since they were too young to go to school they lived in what was called the "baby house". My brothers Floyd and Harry were together in the same area with the "big" boys, and Joan was taken to another area for the "big" girls. Our family was no longer together—we were all separated. I was left all alone without any of my family with me. I felt as if I was totally abandoned by my whole family, especially my sister Joan, she was my big sister. I had all these brothers and sisters, and now nothing but strangers. I had no one. I was alone.

In the morning we got up at six, and an older girl was assigned to look after me. She showed me where to brush my teeth and wash my face. Then she showed me how to make our beds and fold up our pajamas and put them under the pillow. We were also given underwear, socks, undershirts, and nice dresses to wear. At six-thirty, we had to be in the chapel for Mass, which was just up the steps. It was the prettiest chapel I had ever seen. After Mass, we went down this long hall to the dining room. We had to stand at our place at the table and say a prayer. When the nun clapped her hands we were allowed to sit down and eat in silence. If the nun clapped her hands again, we could talk for a while. When she clapped her hands again, we had to be silent. At each table there were maybe six girls, depending on how many children were there at the time. There were some younger and older girls at each table so that the older ones could help the young ones. When we finished eating, we said a prayer, and one of the big girls would bring a dishpan of hot soapy water to the table to wash the dishes. There was one girl washing and two girls drying the dishes, and then they set the table up right away for the next meal.

The orphanage had three floors, with a partial attic on the third floor. The boys had their own bedroom on the third floor and they had their own dining room on the ground level (first floor) along with their bathroom.

The kitchen was also on the first floor along with the girl's playroom, a pantry (where you could buy candy when they opened the doors if you had money) and two bathrooms, one for the girls and one for the nuns. The laundry room was down a long hallway on the first floor. Beyond that there was a cold storage area where they kept all the rolls and donuts that the bakeries would donate in barrels. We would sneak in there and snatch up our favorite roll or donut. There would always be big black ants crawling around in the barrels, but we didn't care and we ate them anyway. They were supposed to be day-old donuts and rolls, but to us they were fresh and delicious.

Past the pantry were the classrooms, with one classroom on each floor. On the first floor was the classroom for the first, second, and third-grade classes combined. On the second floor was a classroom for the fourth and fifth-grade classes. On the third floor the sixth, seventh, and eighth-grade classes shared a classroom. The girls and boys were kept separate from each other except during school and Mass. Sometimes we were lucky if we got to see one of our brothers when we went to school or at Mass in the morning. Floyd and I were in the same grade, so I got to see him, but we really weren't allowed to talk to each other. Rules, rules, rules …

Before I went to the orphanage, I was allowed to start school early since my birthday was in November and because there were so many babies at home. This is why Floyd and I were in the same grade. After I completed the fifth-grade the teacher held me back telling me they didn't want Floyd and me to be in the same class together.

In the beginning, I saw my big sister, Joan, when we went to meals and church. Sometimes she would be allowed to help with the younger ones in the home. We also saw each other on the playground.

At least my two brothers, Floyd and Harry, had each other. The little ones Beverly, Shirley, and Frankie were with each other in the baby house. We got to see them when our mom came to visit, which wasn't very often. She never had a car and had to ride the bus, and she also had a little one, Patty, at home. We would cry and she would cry. She always seemed to be fat but she was probably pregnant then with my brother Ronnie because he was born in May of 1946. Sometimes our grandparents and one or two of our aunts would come to visit and bring some of our cousins with them. We would be running through the great big long halls and they would get to play with us in the boys' play-yard, which we were allowed to do on Sundays when we had visitors. Our mom always had to go talk to the Superior nun in charge because she never paid for our care. Sometimes in the beginning our grandparents would pay.

In the summer, we were allowed to go home one Sunday a month, if they picked us up by one o'clock. We had to be back at the home at five o'clock for supper. Sometimes Grandma and Grandpa would pick us up for our mom, piling seven kids in a little car. We had to sit on the floor and on each other's laps. We were happy to be going home for a while, and Grandma and Grandpa were very good to us.

When Harry started first-grade, Floyd and I were in the third-grade and we were in the same classroom. Harry was always getting beat on the knuckles by our teacher. We all thought she was so mean, and we were all scared of her. I always felt so bad for Harry. I would always cry along with him because it hurt me too.

Our little brother Frankie came to what we called the "big boy's house," when he was only six years old. He was a cute little boy and just a little mischievous. He always seemed to get into trouble so he had to do all the dirty jobs, like cleaning the bathrooms. If he didn't do it right, the nuns would really beat him. They would beat you about the head and neck and the face and just kept hitting you until you thought your body would break in two. Then the nuns would make him clean it all over again. Some of the nuns were huge, especially the nun in charge of the boys. She was a big woman, at least to us kids and he was just a little boy. I knew this happened because I actually saw this nun beating him because I was in the girl's playroom, which was right down the hall from the boy's bathroom.

We all had lots of chores to do. We would have to get on our hands and knees and scrub and wax the long hallways. They had to be spotless. When I was eleven years old I learned how to run an electric floor polisher. We all had to learn. After we mastered learning how to use it we had a lot of fun with it. As long as there were no nuns around, we would let the younger ones sit on it and we would take them for a ride. We were always hoping that we wouldn't get caught or get the little ones hurt.

There were about twenty-eight to thirty beds in the girls' bedroom, about fifteen on each side of the room. Sister Mary Russ, who was in charge of the girls, had her own little cubicle, with a curtain around it for privacy. She also had her own little bathroom. Sometimes we would sneak into her cubicle and get in her medicine cabinet to steal her Aspergum—it was like an aspirin, but it was gum. You weren't allowed to see the nuns without their "habits" (the nuns uniform); it was like some kind of sin if you did. They were especially not allowed to show their hair.

There were a lot of large cupboards in our bedroom, and we each had our own place to keep our dresses and coats. There was one row of cupboards on the bottom and one row across the top that we used to play in. We couldn't get to the top without a stepladder, but there was a window in the middle cupboard and we would go in, shut the door, and climb on the windowsill to get to the upper cupboard to hide sometimes. In some of the cupboards, they stored clothes that we could choose from when we outgrew the ones we were wearing. There was one cupboard that had a lot of beautiful little girls' dresses in it. I don't know why they were there because they were for smaller girls or babies. We always had fun just going through these cupboards and looking at all the tiny dresses because they were so pretty. Another cupboard had winter coats in it and all kinds of shoes we could try on when we needed them. We used to climb in those cupboards too, but we needed a ladder. If we got the ladder out and sister wasn't in there, we would get in trouble for getting it out without permission. There was also a long rod in the middle of the room to hang clothes on. When there was a holiday or special occasion, they would hang our clothes there so they would be ready for us in the morning and we wouldn't have to waste time looking for them. Sometimes we hung our winter coats on the middle rod. We never wore coats that much, because we never had to leave the building to go to school. We only needed them on Sundays when we would go to Mass at the parish church across the street, or if we went home with our family on one Sunday a month, which didn't happen too often. Our play coats were downstairs under the stairway near the girls' playroom, for when we went sledding or played outside.

The nuns were always telling us that the Russians were coming to get us, especially if we were bad or misbehaved. We were always afraid they would get us, so we would make a plan as to how we would hide in the cupboards. There was also a

25

window in the middle bathroom, and we would climb through it sometimes when we were playing. It came out in the hallway where the fourth and fifth-grade classrooms were. Sometimes we would see our brothers there. Sometimes we also saw them behind the building. If someone saw us together, like the handyman or one of the other girls, and they told on us, we would be in trouble. We got in trouble a lot. We were just kids trying have fun and to see our family.

There was a stairway right outside the girls' bedroom that led up to the chapel and down to the basement laundry room. There was also a broom closet at the bottom of this stairway and a long hallway. Sometimes we would hide in there when we would hear one of the nuns coming down the hallway so they wouldn't find something for us to do, or get after us if we did not belong there. We could tell most of the time which nun it was by the sound of their swinging Rosary beads that hung around their waist.

There were two other bathrooms, besides the sisters' bathroom, for the twenty to twenty-eight girls who were there at any one time. We would get a bath and wash our hair once a week. We had a reservoir on the grounds, so we had to use very little water. In summertime, we had to go barefoot all the time, so about five or six of us would all sit around the tub in about six inches of water to get our feet clean before going to bed. We enjoyed it because we would get silly. From May until the first of September, any month without an "R" in it we had to go barefoot except for church and on Sundays. We had to save our shoes.

We woke up at six a.m., washed up, and brushed our teeth with whatever we had: soap, baking soda, or water. Our parents were supposed to bring us toothpaste, but they seldom ever did.

There were twelve small sinks in the middle of the room, six on each side. We were all assigned to a certain sink, sometimes two to a sink. We had one towel and one washcloth each to last us all week, and they had to be hung up neatly under our sinks.

Then we would go upstairs to Mass, where we were instructed ahead of time to be quiet. No coughing or sneezing—you had to hold it back. You would get in trouble for making any noise at all in church. If you didn't sit up perfectly straight or kneel up straight in church, you also got in trouble.

Then we went off to breakfast. Each of us had a small chore to do, and then we went to school. We did have recess time where we went outside if the weather was nice. Otherwise, we stayed in the classroom and read a book.

For lunch, we went to the dining room, and then back to school. After school, we had to change into our play clothes and hang up our school clothes for the next day. We wore our clothes for a week to save on water, so we had to keep them clean. Then we got to go play outside for an hour, unless it was raining; then we would go to the playroom and stay inside and color or play around on the piano. We also played with paper dolls, played tic-tac-toe, or just talked.

We then went to the sewing room for an hour, where Miss Maggie taught us to sew and embroider beautiful pillowcases and little squares for baby quilts. Miss Maggie was an elderly lady that lived in the home on the same floor where the nuns slept. Miss Maggie would put the squares together to make the most beautiful quilts to raffle off at our summer picnics. We also embroidered tablecloths and dresser scarves, whatever Miss Maggie could think of. I learned to sew on the sewing machine when I was nine years old. Once I sewed right through my finger, and they just pulled the needle out and put a bandage on it. It was okay.

We had a talking parrot named Polly Parrot in the sewing room. He would say "hello" when someone came into the room. We would pray before we started to sew, and Polly Parrot would say the Our Father and other prayers along with us. He would also say, "Polly wants a cracker" and swing his head back and forth while singing "La, la, la, la." He was a funny bird. We really enjoyed him. Sometimes when he would hear us pass by, he would squawk and we would go in and talk to him and he would just start singing for us.

The girls were only allowed in certain areas of the third floor. The boy's rooms were up there and we weren't allowed near the boy's area and it was also where the nun's quarters were. We were only allowed to go to the top of the stairs near the nun's quarters because we had to dust the stairs. At the other end of the hall outside the sewing room was a stairway we were allowed to use that went straight up into the attic. At the end of the attic was a door that also led into the boy's bedrooms but it was always kept locked. In the attic we used to stretch freshly washed and starched lace curtains on frames that had nails sticking out all around the frame. We had to be careful so that we didn't get blood on the curtains because you had to put the edges of the curtain over the nails to stretch them. You could stretch at least six curtains on one frame and they would dry really crisp and didn't need ironing. When we finished we would always have pinpricks in our fingers from all the nails.

The Halloween costumes were kept in the attic and it was also where they hid all the Christmas presents for the children. The presents were donated to the orphanage during the year. We knew the presents were there because we would sneak a peek when we had a chance after we got older. There were a lot of ways to get into trouble in the orphanage and this was one of them.

There was a beautiful chapel on the third floor, and we were allowed to go there when it was time for church services. When I got older, I got to clean the chapel and I really enjoyed that. I got to spend some quiet time with Jesus and I knew I couldn't get in trouble because he wouldn't tell on me.

At mealtimes we would stand behind our chairs until we said our prayer. We were not allowed to talk at the table until the sister clapped her hands. If we did, we were bad, which is what they always called us—"bad." I was always bad because I was always in trouble for talking. Sometimes they would send us to the bedroom without eating. After the others finished eating, they would clear the table of leftover food, and they had to carry the leftovers downstairs to be put away. Usually the girls would detour around and come up a back stairway to the girl's bedroom and give us the leftovers before they went to the kitchen. Then they would go to the kitchen, put the leftovers away, and go back to the dining room acting very innocent. I was always sure the nuns knew exactly what we did. It always took us longer to get back. We learned to do that from the older girls. The nuns never said a word. Then we would say our prayer of thanks and set about washing the dishes at the tables. We carried a basin of soapy water to each table. One girl would wash and one would dry the dishes, and then we set the table right away for the next meal.

After we got older, the "big girls" had to go to the kitchen and wash up all the pots and pans. There were some giant-size pots and pans that were almost bigger then we were. We were tiny girls and it was a big job washing them up. I complained a lot and was very sassy, as I got older. I also got smacked around for being sassy and was told to sacrifice it up to the Lord. One time over the summer, we had a new nun that was nice to all of us. She would tease me when I would get angry at all the pots and pans and I got over it fast because she was teasing me.

We had really big cans of fruits and vegetables and after we emptied the cans, we had to open the can on the other end and put both lids in the middle of the opened can and then step on it to smash it flat. This was so that it wouldn't take up so much room in the trash.

On Mondays, we had to help with the laundry—folding sheets, towels, pillowcases, and whatever else had to be folded. Everything had to be folded exactly as we were told, with perfect creases so it took two of us to fold the sheets correctly.

We each had to sew a number into our clothing, socks, underwear, shirts, and pajamas, so they could be sorted out and distributed to the proper person. All of the small clothing—underwear, socks, and pajamas—were kept under our pillows. We never had dresser drawers of our own.

On Tuesdays, we did the ironing. Everything was sprinkled down with water, rolled up, and put in baskets to be ironed. There were mostly dresses and shirts to be ironed, and the nuns showed us exactly how to iron them. First you ironed the collar, and then the yoke, and then the sleeves, front bodice, and back bodice, and then you ironed the body of the shirt. If you didn't do it in order, you got a slap or yelled at, and then the garment got sprinkled and rolled up and put back in the basket to do over. One of the nuns used a steam presser to press the pillowcases and the boys' pants and shirts, and other big stuff. When we got older, we learned to use the steam press, and one time I burned myself on the arm. We ironed until the work was all done—handkerchiefs, dresses, shirts anything they could think of. Four of us at a time did the ironing, and sometimes it took a couple days. I was ironing when they came and told me our mom had her tenth baby, Geraldine.

On Saturday every other week we took the top sheet off of our beds and put it on the bottom mattress and put a clean sheet on the top, and made up the beds nicely. The boys did the same on the opposite weekend so they would not have to wash all the sheets at once. Sometimes during playtime on Friday, some of us bigger girls would sneak up to the bedroom and try to get it done as a surprise for the sister, so it wouldn't have to be done on Saturday. She always acted surprised when we did that to save her time.

When we became of age to have our periods, they never explained anything to us, and neither did our parents. They took us aside and gave us some rags that looked like diapers, and two safety pins, and showed us how to use them. They said, "You will need this once a month, and if you don't use it, you're pregnant." Our mom never told us anything about it either, it was like it was bad and you did not discuss it. We knew our mom had babies, but we never asked her how. No one ever explained it. Once I missed my period, and I was scared to death I was pregnant. I couldn't imagine how it happened. I never told anyone. I just worried for three months, and then I finally got my period again. Boy, was I relieved.

On Halloween, we always had a Halloween party in the girls' dining room. The big girls were allowed to go to the attic and rummage through the costumes and select what they wanted to wear, as long as the sister said it was okay. At the party, we would parade in front of the superior nun and she judged best costume. Every year the same kid won and was voted best costume. She and her twin brother were only a few weeks old when they were brought to the home along with their two older siblings. The nuns cared for them as if they were their own children because both of their parents were dead. They were treated as very special children.

After we were at the orphanage for a while, we were referred to as "the Crawfords." We were treated very mean by some of the sisters and we felt it was because our parents never paid for us to be there and also because we had "two parents" where some of the children at the home had only one parent or none at all. Some of the sisters actually called us "Trash". Everyone knew who we were because there were so many of us, seven at this time, and we all look alike. It was always, "Oh, those are the *Crawfords*" and I grew to hate that name.

At Thanksgiving dinner, there was a cream soda by each plate on the table. We never had soft drinks any other time. We always drank milk, water, Kool-Aid, or lemonade, which was fine—we liked it. The cream soda was a great treat, and it dressed up the tables for the holiday. We were all very excited because it looked so pretty on the tables.

Christmas was the best time of the year. On St. Nick's day, candy would magically appear in the classroom like it came from nowhere. It just came flying across the room. (We found out after we left the orphanage that one of the nuns would get up on a ladder and throw it through the transom above the doors.) At lunchtime they would march us through the halls singing Christmas carols until we got to our dining room, and there at our places were huge Santa Claus cookies that barely fit on our plate along with candy and fruit. It was a very special time because I really loved singing.

At Christmas, we would always go to a lot of parties. We would go to the Beverly Hills Supper Club in Southgate, where we saw a live show, had lunch, got a gift, played games, and received some candy to take back home. We also would go to the Hippodrome Theatre in the city, where we played games and they would put on a show and give us a bag of candy. The year I was thirteen, I won a really big bride doll. She was the most beautiful thing I ever owned. I won the doll by playing the game where you put a marshmallow on a string and wrap the string around your tongue and get the marshmallow in your mouth. I was the first one to get the marshmallow in my mouth and I won. I loved that doll.

We would also go to the elementary school in the area. It was only a couple of blocks from the orphanage. They would have a play for us and give us candy. Sometimes if one of us was bad, we didn't get to go. We had to stay at the orphanage.

Sometimes we would go to one of our classrooms that had a big screen set up in it and watch a movie. We saw several Shirley Temple movies, *Heidi and The Little Colonel*. We also saw *The Man in the Iron Mask, The Song of Bernadette*, and *Our Lady Of Fatima*. Sometimes if the movie wasn't due back, they would actually let us see it again if we were good. We enjoyed the chance to watch it over again.

I was ten years old when I had to have my tonsils taken out, along with my sister Shirley and two other girls. We went to St. Elizabeth North Hospital, and they took one of us at a time to surgery. When they brought my sister back, she looked to me like she was dead. She was so skinny and frail anyway, and that scared me to death. I was afraid to have my tonsils taken out, because the three other girls also came back looking dead. When they tried to put me to sleep, I fought them off something awful, but they won. When they brought me back to my room, they had to take me right back to the operating room because my throat was bleeding like crazy. The stitches had come apart, and they had to stitch it back up. I would try to talk, and it wouldn't come out right. That was my first time ever being in the hospital. We spent a few days in bed at the orphanage eating Jell-O, soup and ice cream, which was the only good part about that surgery.

One Sunday, our dad took us to the zoo. He worked there in the penny arcade, and he gave us pennies to play. Well, when we got back to the orphanage, we told a visiting nun that we went to the zoo. When Sister Russ came along, she told the visiting nun, "Don't believe a word the Crawfords say, they are all liars. Their dad doesn't work." (It was true that most of the time he didn't.) I was really hurt. I knew what we did, and I was not lying. Our parents had lied to the nuns about working. They just thought our dad never worked because he never paid for us. That was the last time our dad ever came to visit us. Our mom had told the sisters that he was not allowed to visit anymore. We never knew why she told them that because she was still married to him.

There were lots of times when the nuns would speak to each other in German, especially Sister Russ, so that we would not understand what they were saying. We figured they were saying something about one of us that they didn't want us to hear when we would hear someone's name mentioned in the conversation.

In the bedroom at night, if we talked it was bad, and I was always bad. I was always talking, and Sister Russ would make me sit on the chapel steps right outside our bedroom door. When the other sisters would go up to chapel to say their prayers before bed, they would see me sitting on the steps, and as each one passed by me she would say, "Bad again, huh?"

There were a couple of nuns who taught at the grade school across the street from the orphanage and they lived there in separate nuns' quarters because it was close to where they worked. They also had a study where they could do their homework for school and they would also help watch the children on the week-ends.

I was scared to death of the thunder and lightning. Once there was a really bad storm, and because I was always bad, sister made me sleep in the last bed in the corner of the room. There was a huge heavy metal door that rattled in the wind all the time. When it stormed it was much worse, and I was so scared I would cry myself to sleep.

Then there were times at night when I couldn't sleep, and I would count the pretty embossed metal squares on the ceiling or pray the Rosary. They told us if we started the Rosary and didn't finish it, our Guardian Angel would finish it for us if we fell asleep.

One time I was really bad and I did deserve to be punished. My sister Patty was visiting from the baby house, and I couldn't be outside with her because I had some work I had to finish. So I brought her in with me and one of the sisters came along and told Patty she had to go outside to play. When the sister walked away, I told Patty that she didn't have to listen to the nuns, because I was her big sister. Sister heard me, and she beat the holy hell out of me. She slapped me around the face, neck, head, shoulders, and back until I sunk to the floor. It was my own fault I shouldn't have said that to Patty. What was worse was that one of the other girls stood there and watched while she beat me.

There were other times, when someone did something bad and no one would own up to it and we all got in trouble. The nun would line us all up and one by one we got a spanking. It was misery waiting in that line until it was your turn. I know I was always hoping she would be too tired when it was my turn, but no such luck.

When I was in the sixth grade, I talked out of turn to the sister during class. She called me up to the front of the class, which was sixth- seventh- and eighth-grade boys and girls together. She pulled up my dress and beat me with a belt in front of the whole class. I was totally humiliated and ashamed. I never wanted to face anyone ever again. I hated her.

Chapter 3

In the summer of 1950, I was going into the seventh-grade when school started. Sister Angel came to work at the orphanage to watch us on the playground and to be our seventh-grade teacher. She was the most wonderful nun of all. She was a very kind, gentle, sweet, and compassionate nun. She treated us like children, not dogs. To her, we were not *the Crawfords*; we were all children of God.

One day after class, she took me aside and talked to me like I was someone who was to be treated like a person. She respected us, which was surprising. She was the first really nice nun. There were a couple of nuns who came in the summertime who were nice, but they didn't stay. They just came to watch us in the summer. It was like they were on vacation. Sister Angel told me that I was a very pretty girl, and she encouraged me to make myself look better by fixing my hair and putting a little curl in it. She told me I would feel a lot better about myself. She even put her arm around my shoulder. No one ever did anything like that to me before. They were really not allowed to touch us, except to hit us. We were told by one nun that the sisters were not allowed to touch us and be comforting to us in any way, because it would make them want to have children of their own. So touching was off limits. It was also off limits for us kids to even hold hands with the girl standing next to you when you were lined up to go to class or to dinner we were told that was bad. Almost everything we did seemed to be bad.

I listened to Sister Angel and curled my hair nicely with rags or metal strips that came on the coffee bags to seal them. We would tie the rags or strips around some hair and rolled it up tight, and in the morning you would have curly hair. I wasn't good at it because I had never done it before. But I did it, and when I came to class the next time, she actually complimented me in front of the whole class. I was so embarrassed, but it felt good. She really cared about us. I do not ever remember hearing our mom telling us that we were pretty, but this sister did. I felt special that day, and I did look better. Up to this point we had never been encouraged to really care about our appearance.

It was around this time that I was old enough to really begin to appreciate the value of prayer and talking to Jesus. It was just he and I. I could cry to him and tell him everything and not get in trouble for talking too much—unlike when we would tell our mom when they beat on us. In the beginning our mom would go to the superior nun and talk to her about the nuns hitting on us. Then we would get into trouble again with the nuns for telling, so we learned the hard way not to tell our mom when we would get beat or get in trouble. I did learn that I could only trust talking to Jesus. He became my only hope, and it was a big help. I would always feel better after I talked to him.

On All Souls Day, November 2nd, they would leave the doors from the playground to the chapel open so we could run up to the third floor to the chapel to say prayers for the poor souls in heaven. Every time we made a visit to the chapel and said a prayer, we were told that we got some poor soul out of Purgatory, and we would gain indulgences for these poor souls.

When we were allowed out to play, we had swings on the playground, a merry-go-round, and three great big trees with sandboxes built around them. We could sit for what seemed like hours and built sandcastles with cars going into tunnels around those big trees. We would swing on those swings until we were swinging so high we were even with the bars on top. We were lucky not to have gotten hurt. It was scary. Sometimes we would have a mishap, like a little kid walking too close to a swing and getting hit with the swing, but nothing serious.

We had three bicycles on the girls' side, in three different sizes, but we had to take turns. They were stored in what used to be a smokehouse right in the middle of the girls' playground. One time my little sister Shirley got locked in the smokehouse by accident. She was already afraid of almost anything since she was kidnapped when she was three years old, and that made things worse for her. There were a lot of squabbles over those bikes, because we all liked to ride them.

We would do a lot of jumping rope, and we were very good at jumping double-dutch. Everyone loved to jump rope. If we got roller skates for Christmas, it was another fun thing for us to do on the playground. Everyone wanted a turn, so there was some bickering over the skates. Of course, sometimes we had to man the brooms and sweep the playground down. We would form a line across the top of the playground and sweep until the end. We would sweep all the leaves over the hill and pick up any trash along the way. We would get blisters on our hands, but the grounds looked pretty good afterward. When it would snow, we had a few sleds to take turns with, and George, our handyman, would always find us some cardboard boxes to use for sledding. They worked pretty well for a while, until they got too wet, and by that time it was time to go back inside.

On the grounds of the orphanage was a road that led past the barns and fruit trees out to a little old chapel in the open field. Sometimes the Sisters would pack a small picnic lunch, and we would walk back to this chapel. We would go into the chapel and say a few prayers and then we would have our picnic on the ground outside the chapel.

The orphanage was also a working farm with a great big barn. My brothers and the other boys had to work it. They had cows the boys would milk, and if we happened to walk by when they were milking, they would aim it at us and give us a squirt of milk. They also had to feed the chickens and horses and slop the pigs. Like all the rest of us, they were kept busy. When it came time to kill the chickens, they would have to help chop off the heads, pluck the feathers, and get the birds ready to cook.

George, our handy man, also ran the big machines in the laundry room for us and helped out on the farm and wherever he was needed at the Home. He and his wife had both grown up in the orphanage. He had four children and his wife would bring them to the orphanage to visit. His children were adorable and they were always dressed nicely. Of course, the nuns were happy to see them when they would visit. George also took us to the dentist and other places that we needed to be driven to. Every time he would drive us somewhere and we would go under the underpass in the city, he would always holler, "Here we go, under the underpants." We thought it was so funny. He was a really nice man and was always telling jokes. He liked to see us smile. He was good to us because he knew what it was like to have to grow up in the orphanage.

At times we had a doctor who would come to the orphanage and treat us when someone was sick. Dr. Ragan was a very nice doctor and he would line us up for shots, which we hated. There was a time when we had an epidemic of diphtheria; lots of the children were very sick. My sister and I, along with several other children, were sent to what they called the infirmary because we had symptoms of the disease. The infirmary was located on the first floor of the "baby-house" near the boys' playroom and the babies lived on the second floor. This was a sad time because we had lost a little five-year-old boy to the disease.

George always had the job of bringing the cows' heads to the kitchen after they were butchered. The nuns were going to make something with them, like turtle soup sometimes. If we were in the kitchen at the time, George would say to us, "Look into the cow's eyes and see what the cow saw last." Naturally we would, and it would be our own reflection. He thought that was so funny, and of course we did too.

We always had an annual summer picnic that helped support the orphanage. The week of the picnic we had to clean hundreds of chickens that would be served at the picnic. The "big" girls would gather around two long tables in the laundry room along with a few of the nuns and we cleaned the guts out and took the "yellowsocks" off of all of the chickens. We also had to make sure there were no "pin-feathers" left on the chickens, and then we put them in tubs of cold water to soak. One nun was the inspector to make sure we did a good job. Before we started working, we would say a few prayers and the Rosary then we would sing some songs. We were allowed to talk unless we got too rowdy, and then the nuns would clap their hands for us to be quiet.

The picnics were a lot of fun where we got to run around, and if any of our family members would come, we could spend time with them. We also got to take turns serving in the cafeteria. The girls carried trays for the visitors as they came through the line for dinners. We had our little aprons on and were told to be very polite and smile. We had to show the visitors that we were well behaved. We enjoyed serving in the cafeteria because we got to meet lots of people, and they were very nice to each of us. Sometimes they would give us a tip, and we were allowed to keep that money. The day after the picnic, we had to go down to the picnic area and clean up the grounds. Any money we found while cleaning up we also got to keep, and buy candy in our pantry during the week.

On the Fourth of July, we would go the "Mother House", which was the home for all the nuns, where they had their annual festival to raise money for their order. We would work the festival for them. We would carry trays for the visitors and help where we could. We also got tips there. The very next day, they took us back again to help clean up the grounds. That was always a lot of fun. We got to see the sisters who came in the summertime, who were good to us. It was also fun because we got to go somewhere else away from the orphanage for a while.

When we were older we had to work in the kitchen and helped out with the cooking and cleaning. Once I was told by the sister in charge of the kitchen to wash the butter. It came white from the farm, and we were told we had to wash the salt out of it and to put a color in it to make it yellow. I turned on the water, and I accidentally turned on the hot-water faucet. I turned it off right away as soon as I realized what I had done, but the sister had already seen me. She started screaming at me and started beating me with her big old fists all about my head and neck. She beat the holy hell out of me. She was a very tall and heavy set nun. I didn't think she would ever stop pounding on me. After that I had to continue with washing the butter and I cried my eyes out the whole time. From them on, I always made sure I paid close attention and stayed away from the hot-water faucet.

One Thanksgiving, my younger sister was told to cut up celery and put it in the dressing, but she accidentally put it in the sweet potatoes instead. She got into big trouble for that one too.

The sisters used to get a special breakfast on Sundays, and it always smelled so good to us. I always wished we could have what they were having especially when it was bacon. One day I saw something strange looking on their plates, and they told me that it was cow's tongue, I was so glad I was not a nun that day, because I wouldn't have eaten it.

Besides George, the handyman, there was another man who worked the farm for the orphanage. He lived in a nice little house on the property near the barn, and about once a month two of us girls had to walk down and clean up his place real good for him. We were all very leery of going to his place, because he was a stranger to us. We hardly ever saw him, but he was very kind to us when we would run into him.

The boys dug potatoes and picked apples, pears, peaches, green beans, cucumbers, and whatever else they grew on the farm. In the summer, we would go down to the dining hall, were they cooked and served the dinners for the picnics. The dining hall was about a half a block away from the orphanage. It was a really long dining hall, with a huge kitchen where they cooked and canned all the food grown on the farm. There were long tables set up where we would prepare all the fruits and vegetables for canning—snapping beans and peeling peaches and pears. We would get all sticky, with juice from the fruit running down our arms, and it t was a very messy job. We also snapped messes and messes of green beans. They would dump bushel baskets full of beans on the table, and we would look at the mounds of beans like we would never get finished, but we always did. It was fun because we had something different to do, and we would sing songs and pray the Rosary.

The sisters, along with the help of the older boys, canned everything that we were getting ready for them. They had all the right equipment they needed to do the canning. While they were canning they would even put food coloring in the pears, some red for Valentine's Day and some green for St. Patrick's Day. We always thought that was pretty neat. By the time the holidays came along, we had forgotten all about the special fruit that was made for the occasion and we were pleasantly surprised by our dessert. Some of the fruits and vegetables were also used for the festival. Those canning days were long and hard, and I am sure they were hard for the nuns also. After all, the nuns were older than we were, and if we were tired I am sure that they were also tired.

When all the canning was done, the jars were taken to the cellar, which was under the baby house. This was a separate building from the main building. To us, the cellar looked like the catacombs, or a dungeon with lots of spider-webs. It had a dirt floor and mazelike rooms to roam through to find what you were looking for. Throughout the year, the nuns would send us over to get certain fruits and vegetables. None of us liked to go there because it was very scary and spooky to us. It was like going underground.

When we got older, we were allowed to go to the baby house and watch the little ones or play with them. This was one of my favorite things to do. I got to help care for my little brother and sisters. When I was eleven years old, my three younger siblings—Patty, Ronnie and Gerry—were brought to the orphanage. The orphanage had made an exception by taking Gerry at the age of fourteen months. They normally didn't take children in before the age of two. We thought it was strange that our mom would have more babies when there were already seven of us in the Home. By the time she was twenty-eight years old, she had ten kids who were all in an orphanage. I don't know what she was thinking.

At the orphanage we had nice clean beds to sleep in and lots of good food. We got a good education but my brothers and sisters and I hardly ever felt loved. We didn't feel like anyone cared for us. Even though there were lots of us, we still felt alone but we survived it all.

I enjoyed being with my younger siblings; we hardly ever got to see them. I was third oldest in the family, and I loved playing with and taking care of the babies. In the baby house, they had these tiny little toilets. They looked like little potty chairs, only they were real toilets. All the little ones could go in and use them all by themselves as soon as they learned how. It was cute to see them sitting there doing their business all together when the nuns were training them. They would take them in all together so they would learn. They were just babies. It was funny but cute at the same time. There were times when, if one of the babies were sick and keeping the sister up at night, they would allow me or one of the bigger girls to spend the night just in case they woke up so the sister could get her sleep. I didn't mind. I loved babies already, and we were used to watching them. We were good at it.

The nuns liked to take us on long walks in the spring, which I really enjoyed. They would give us a bag of hard candy and walk us down this road, about three blocks away. The road was at least a mile and a half long and ended near the river. In May, on

Ascension Thursday, we would walk down a different road that had creeks along the side of it. The water in the creeks would be high all the way down the road because of the rains at that time of year. It was always a long hard walk back up the hill. There was candy all over the road from where some of the little ones would fall and drop their candy on the way down. It was always a beautiful day. And we enjoyed it—at least I did. I loved walking.

When I was about twelve, another nun came to the orphanage to be our new cook. She was a very warm friendly person. She was very kind, and she treated us really nice. We found out that she had gone to school with our mom, and she also knew us when we were small. I was sassy and talked back to her, but she just teased me about it. She could handle me and eventually we got along great. She was so good to us. She never laid a hand on me, even though I always expected to get smacked around. She was so patient with us and always very sweet.

It was about that time that another nun, Sister Ina, came to the orphanage. She had actually grown up in the home when she was a young girl. She worked in the laundry room and showed us all exactly how to iron and fold clothes her way. Sometimes she worked in the kitchen and did the cooking. She would make us snow ice cream with nuts in it in the winter and was always sneaking us treats. She was a big, chubby, and kind nun who was very good to us girls. At least that's what we all thought when she first came to serve at the orphanage. One day, when almost everyone was down at the picnic area working on cleaning fruits and vegetables for canning, I was elected to stay and do some ironing. It was just Sister Ina and myself. We were talking as we worked, and then all of a sudden she had grabbed me in a viselike grip from behind, and I was stunned. She was grabbing me all over, touching my body in places where I hated to touch myself (they told us it was a sin) and grabbing my breasts.

The whole time while I was struggling to get away from her, I couldn't talk. I was so shocked by what she was doing to me. I just kept struggling to get away from her, but she held me so

43

tight I couldn't get free. Her arms reached all the way around me, and she was so strong. And she constantly kept asking me to do something to her. I thought she had gone crazy or something—I didn't know what happened to her. She had never done anything like this to me before.

I kept thinking I must have been a horrible person for someone to do this to me. I knew I was bad, but not bad enough for what was happening to me right now. Just as suddenly as she grabbed me, she let me go. We both went about our business like nothing happened, and nothing was said. I was petrified to tell anyone what happened. Then it happened again and again, and I was getting more and more scared every time it happened. It went on and on for over three months. I knew what she was doing to me had to be a sin—a really horrible sin—especially if it was a sin just to hold hands with a little girl standing next to you.

One day I got up the nerve to tell the priest in confession what had happened to me. And he just told me, "You have to remember that sister has a problem, and you need to pray for her." I went away from there more puzzled than ever, thinking *"What about me?"* I felt like I had the bigger problem than she did because I knew it was going to happen again and again—and it did.

During this time I just kept praying and thinking, *"What am I doing to cause this terrible thing to happen to me?"* I had nowhere to turn, if I told another nun, I would probably have gotten beaten and called a liar. I just couldn't figure out what I was doing wrong. I prayed that the Lord would give me an answer. I couldn't get away because I lived at the orphanage night and day. It was horrible. I just couldn't imagine how I got so terribly bad. I thought I was the worst person in the world. It didn't dawn on me to blame Sister Ina. After all I thought she was a good person and it must be my fault. They were always calling me bad anyway, so I was sure that it had to be my fault.

After this all happened, I became very complacent. No more talking back. I even tried to be a better person. I prayed to Jesus a lot more and tried to figure things out, but there was never an answer. One day at school, my teacher, Sister Angel, called me up to the front of the class and asked me to stay in at recess. I was scared—I didn't know what I did again. She was very sweet, and she talked to me very gently. She asked me what was wrong. She told me that she thought I had a problem, and she wanted to talk to me about it. She was so gentle that she got it out of me. I cried my eyes out as I told her the whole story about what sister did to me and how often she did it. I also told her what I had told the priest and what he had said to me in confession, she was not happy about what the priest had said. Apparently he was not allowed to tell anyone because of the seal of confession. I didn't realize that back then and that's probably why it hadn't stopped. Sister Angel continued to talk with me and told me it was not my fault—I was not to blame and that Sister Ina had no business touching me like that at all. She would see to it that it stopped right away and that it would never happened again. And Thank God it did stop. But I could never forget the fact that I must have really been a very bad person anyway for this to actually happen to me.

I missed my whole recess, but I didn't care I felt better hoping that it would never happen again. Later that day after my meeting with Sister Angel, I ran into Sister Russ and she yelled at me for being late for something. She then accused me of telling her favorite young girl that there was no Santa Claus, and she beat the holy hell out of me. She beat me about the head, neck, and face until I fell to the floor, crying the whole time she was beating me. It hurt much worse because I knew I didn't do what she accused me of. Apparently she had asked Sister Angel why I was so late for recess, and because Sister Angel didn't want to reveal exactly what we discussed, she told Sister Russ that I had told one of her favorite girls there was no Santa Claus, she told her she had talked to me about not telling any of the younger children about Santa again. Sister Angel didn't know that Sister Russ would beat me for that and I never told Sister Angel what she did. I decided to keep my mouth shut. After the beating I figured it was a good punishment for what I caused Sister Ina to do to me when I was only twelve years old. I didn't understand or know what it was all about and I couldn't imagine someone ever doing that kind of thing to anyone.

After I had my talk with Sister Angel, Sister Ina never touched me again. And it was never mentioned again by anyone, especially Sister Ina. Whenever I was near the laundry room alone and would hear Sister Ina coming down the hall, I would hide in the broom closet at the bottom of the steps. They all made a different noise when they walked. We had pretty many of them figured out so we wouldn't get in trouble. After a while, I kind of just put it out of my mind and actually forgot about it until I was much older. The memories were too horrendous. Not long after that incident, Sister Ina was sent away.

Sometimes children only came to the orphanage for a short time. Maybe their mom or dad would be sick or dying, and they didn't have to stay very long. Some of the girls in that situation would run away. They knew where they were and knew how to get back to their home. We didn't. We had no clue as to where we were, and we were afraid to leave. We didn't go home enough to know where we were. The nuns were always threatening us that they would send us to the bad girls' home in the city if we did try to run away. They told us that the nuns there were really mean. We didn't want to run away from the orphanage, we thought some of the nuns we had were mean enough already.

We had spelling contests in school, and competed to be able to get to go to the Cincinnati Gas and Electric Co. for a spelldown with all the schools in our area. There weren't too many students in our seventh and eighth grade classes and I was a very good speller. I won that spelling contest and got to go to the spelldown. Whoever won there would go to Washington, DC, for the finals. I was third last and almost made it to the end, but I never won. The word I missed on was "obstacle." When they pronounced the word, it sounded like they said "obsticle," and I wasn't thinking and I misspelled it. Still, I was excited about being able to participate. Our mom even came to watch, and I got my picture in the newspaper. I was so happy that I did something well and I was the top speller for my school.

We had a choir when I was in seventh grade. I had a decent voice and I loved to sing and I was selected as one of the choir members. Our mother always sang and she had a beautiful voice. My two younger sisters were able to join when they got old enough. I really enjoyed singing, and they told us that singing was twice praying. We sang for all the special holidays: Christmas, Easter, and Forty Hours Devotion. Forty Hours Devotion was a three-day adoration of the Blessed Sacrament, and then on Sunday we sang at the closing. It was a big celebration. All the girls wore white dresses and veils and we led the Blessed Sacrament to the altar in procession. Lots of priests would come for this special occasion. We got to serve them a fancy dinner in the girls' dining room. It was actually exciting for us. On the night before we sang, Sister Russ would let us stay up later and have some relaxing time and some hot lemonade. She served us hot lemonade so our singing pipes would be in good working order. She also did this for us when we sang for Christmas and Easter. We enjoyed the hot lemonade and the time to stay up later with Sister.

When we were thirteen and fourteen, we were allowed to stay up later and have "adult" time to just sit around and talk. We felt like grownups.

In the summertime, they would take us to a swimming pool that also had a playground. The place was called Martz Grove and it was in Ross, Kentucky. Some of us girls hated that we had to undress and put on bathing suits to swim. We felt naked and were ashamed to show our body. One of the first things we were taught when we first came to the orphanage was how to dress and undress while changing into our pajamas without showing any part of our body.

At Martz Grove every year, the nuns would tell us the same story—"Stay away from the river—because, one year, one of the girls went too close to the river and fell in and drowned". So we were afraid of going down the little hill to the river. The boys would go to the river, though; they weren't afraid of anything.

There was also a ball field and a lot of swings, and even mechanical ones that we had to take turns on. There was a huge cafeteria where they would serve us a good meal and we could get a drink.

Also in the summer we got to ride on the Island Queen riverboat. We would take a bus to the public landing in Cincinnati where we would get on the Island Queen. It was a paddleboat that took you down the river to Coney Island, but I hated boats. I remember one time when our mom took us out on the licking River, in a really small boat, along with her then, giant-sized boy friend. They were trading places in the boat, right in the middle of the Licking River, and the boat was rocking so hard we thought we were all going to fall into the river. None of us could swim, and all of us girls were crying.

Once we got moving on the Island Queen, we forgot all about being on a boat. There were fun things to do on the boat, and they kept us busy until we reached Coney Island. We had a lot of fun at Coney Island. We were all dressed nice like we were going to church. We had to wear nametags of a certain color because it was Orphanage Day at Coney. The different orphanages each wore a certain color so they could keep track of you better. We ran in groups of five and rode all the rides we could, even the wild ones. I liked the one called the Wildcat. We would see who could ride it the most times. Then they would serve us lunch. We ran some more after that, and at six o'clock, we got back on the Island Queen and rode back to Cincinnati. A lot of the little ones fell asleep on the way back. It was an exciting day for everyone, and we were all wore out.

The Parish Church just across the street had a wonderful, warm, and very kind pastor. He would come over and visit with us. Sometimes he would throw his hat in one door (they wore the miter hats) and then come to the other door, and he would ask if we had seen his twin brother. We would laugh and say no. He never had a twin brother, and we knew it. Sometimes he would come to have breakfast at the orphanage. The nuns would set him up in the fancy dining room, but he would always bring his plate and sit at our table and eat with all of us girls. He was a very kind priest. He would tell jokes and tease us all the time.

In the kitchen, we had a huge walk-in refrigerator that we called the walk-in box. It had a glass window in it so you could look in to see what you needed without opening the door. Sometimes we would sneak in when we thought no one else was around and swipe peaches, pears, Jell-O, or whatever we could get a hold of to eat without getting caught. The sister who did the cooking would make Goetta all the time, (Goetta is a breakfast dish made from pin-head oats, ground beef and ground sausage that is popular in the Northern Kentucky area) it was very good and most of us really loved it. It was one of our main staples. We always had lots of good food at the orphanage compared to what we had to eat before we came to the orphanage. We had lots of good fresh milk that came straight from the cows at the orphanage. The farm hands would bring the milk to the kitchen in large silver containers that were about two feet high and put them in the walk-in fridge. We would skim off the cream on top and save it for the nuns for their coffee. Then we would fill pitchers with the milk and take them up to our tables. Not all of the girls liked the milk, including one of my sisters. Since we had to drink all of our milk, I was always finishing up their milk for them so they wouldn't get into trouble. Milk was one of my favorite drinks.

There was this adorable little girl at the orphanage that hated oatmeal. The nuns made her eat it anyway. She would throw it up every time, and they would make her eat it again. They would tell her if she didn't eat it, she would have to eat it for her lunch. Of course it was gone when we went in for lunch, thank God. That is definitely not what my brothers and sisters, and I would have done. We knew what it was like to go hungry and to not know where our next bite of food was coming from, so we never had a problem eating whatever was served.

When we were in the eighth grade we would make our confirmation. Of course, the nuns told us that the bishop would slap us in the face. None of us liked that idea. We were also told to choose a saint's name for our confirmation. I chose Margaret because of a special person named Margaret at the orphanage. The bishop barely touched our cheeks, but the sisters sure knew how to make us behave better by telling us that he was going to slap us.

On the first day in May we always had May Crowning. It was a celebration for our Blessed Mother Mary and since it was such a special occasion, the church was always decorated beautifully. I was the only girl in the sixth, seventh and eighth grade class and an eighth grade girl was always chosen to crown Mary. For several years, it was well talked about that I would get to crown the Blessed Mother. In March of my eighth grade year another girl came to the orphanage. The Sisters decided that since there were two of us, we had to draw names to see who would get to do the crowning. It didn't matter that I had been told that I would get to crown Mary for the past several years. So we drew names, and her name was chosen. I was devastated, and I cried for days. I thought I would never quit crying. I was so upset all the time. I knew what a privilege it was to crown Mary, and now I didn't get to do it.

One day the new girl came to me and told me she didn't want to crown the Blessed Virgin Mary and if it was okay with the Sisters, she would let me do it. I was never so happy and I hugged her. She was so sweet and we remained friends after we left the orphanage. (Years later she asked me to be godmother to her first son.) I felt bad that I was such a baby about the May Crowning, but it was something I had dreamed of for years. Sister Russ even let me wear the same dress that my older sister Joan had worn for her graduation. My grandma had made this dress for Joan and it was beautiful. It was made out of nylon dotted swiss, and I loved it.

Our mom and my older sister Joan, who had already left the orphanage, were there for the May Crowning and after the ceremony they took pictures. After the ceremony was over, the Sister Superior told me that my dress was immodest and was not decent enough to wear in church in front of Jesus. I thought this dumb, because Joan wore it for her graduation two years earlier in that same chapel. It was too late, though—the ceremony was over. Anyway, Sister Russ thought it was perfect. The May Crowning was the highlight of my eighth-grade year. Later that month, I graduated from the eighth grade with one other girl and one boy.

All ten of us on my 8th grade graduation day,
with our mom and Grandparents, May, 1952

Chapter 4

Once you graduated from the eighth grade, you had to leave the orphanage. As it got closer to my graduation, I would get upset, and I cried a lot because I was going to miss everybody especially my family and even some of the nuns. I did not want to leave. This was the only real home I knew. I didn't know what was out there, and I was afraid to go into a strange world. We were not taught about the outside world. The only thing I remembered was what we didn't have before we had to go into the Home. They never prepared us for what to expect in the outside world away from the orphanage.

I never got to go home with our mom, sister, and brother after my graduation. The nuns said that my mom wasn't fit to take care of me, so they sent me to live with a really nice and wealthy Jewish family in Ohio. My older sister and brother, Joan and Floyd, got to go home with our mom, what was wrong with me going home too? I was very upset, but I had to obey because I didn't have a choice, and apparently our mom did not care because she allowed it. I was only fourteen years old and our mom couldn't even say that she wanted me and that she would keep me herself. I wondered what was wrong with me, and why didn't she want me? I also didn't understand why I was being sent to live with a Jewish family, because we were always told we shouldn't associate with people of different faiths.

The orphanage made all the arrangements and sent me to live with this Jewish family. I had to go to a private religious high school a few blocks from their home. When I got there, I was told I would go to school and help watch their four-year-old daughter when I wasn't in school. I was told I also had to clean the house and cook their meals. In the morning before I went to school, I had to dust everything in the downstairs of the house. They had ten rooms in all, with four bathrooms. I had my own little room and bathroom. I would finish cleaning in the afternoon when I came home from school. It was okay living there, but the little girl would always call me "the Witch of Borneo," and I hated that. I was not a witch. The lady of the house, Mrs. Ivy, would give me two dollars for my lunches for the week and to catch the bus on Sunday to visit my family. She would say, "Go to church and then you can catch the bus to visit your family and be home by five o'clock." After a while, I learned to skip church and go earlier to visit my family so I could spend more time with them. She never knew I didn't go to church because I walked to the church and caught the bus right there. I never knew anyone at that church and always felt funny going there. Anyway, it gave me an extra hour with my family. Sometimes we would go to the orphanage and visit with my younger brothers and sisters. That was always really nice but I had to be back at the Ivy's' house by five o'clock. Learning to ride the buses was really hard. I had never done that before.

Since leaving the orphanage, I was always afraid and not secure anymore. I had been at the orphanage for a long time and it was easy because I knew what was expected of me.

In October of that year, Mrs. Ivy had another little girl. I loved babies, so it was okay for a while helping out and doing all that I had to do. I was use to taking orders anyway. When the baby was born, Mrs. Ivy never came down the stairs for two weeks. There was one time when I was fixing lunch; she thought I was taking too long just to make a few sandwiches. She got on the intercom and told me to throw it all out and start over. Then she told me exactly how to make it step by step and no other way. "Lay out the bread, spread with mayo, put on the meat, and then close and cut." It had to be done her way. Then I would carry it upstairs to her and her daughter.

In November of that year, Mrs. Ivy gave me a "party" for my fifteenth birthday. I was allowed to invite two girls from school for an hour. She served tuna sandwiches and Kool-Aid. My friends didn't stay long, and I didn't get any presents, which was fine. I felt terrible for my friends. That wasn't much of a party, but I guess she did the best she could.

Mrs. Ivy had a lady come in once a week who did the washing and ironing. So I never had to do that job, just everything else. All Mrs. Ivy ever did was go out and shop. Her husband was a very nice man, and she was always fussing with him. He seemed to work hard.

One day when I was at school I felt really sick, but it never entered my mind to miss school. When I got home and got to the door of my room, I passed out cold. I was on the floor when they came home, and I guess someone put me in the bed because I awoke to see a doctor standing over me and talking to me. The doctor had come to the house. Later, Mrs. Ivy took me to see the doctor. I never really knew what was wrong with me, but I guess it was female problems. The doctor said when I got married and had a baby, it would clear up. Other than that, I never really got sick and I never passed out again.

One time I had to go to the dentist. Mrs. Ivy gave me instructions on how to catch the bus and go into Cincinnati. Trying to catch a bus to downtown Cincinnati was frightening. I knew nothing about the area, and I was very afraid to take that trip all alone. We were always warned about talking to strangers, and were always told the Russians were coming after us and we might not get back to our families. I was across the river and all alone, and I was afraid that I would never find my way back home. I was petrified, but I survived.

After a while, I hated it there at the Ivy's' home. I was uncomfortable at the school I was attending, and I hardly knew anyone. Mrs. Ivy would not let me go to any football games when someone would ask me. I was not allowed out with any friends in the evenings at all. She would say she wouldn't even let her own little girl go out in the evenings either when she got old enough.

There was a nun at the high school from a different order who taught sewing class. When she would measure me, she would keep running her fingers under the tape across my breasts. It seemed like it would take her forever and I felt very uncomfortable. It frightened me for some reason and I just wanted to get away from her.

I was also uncomfortable in gym class, because you had to put on a short outfit that I hated. I had never worn shorts or pants before, and I felt very naked. I was embarrassed to be dressed like that, but all the other girls never minded it. I hated gym class.

There was one particularly sweet nun at the high school that really seemed to watch over me. I think she thought that I looked too skinny and hungry. She was always sneaking me cookies and treats at lunch, she wanted to fatten me up.

When I turned sixteen, our mom said I had quit school and go to work. I was happy to be leaving the Ivy's' home and that school. When I was getting ready to leave their home I wasn't very nice to Mrs. Ivy, or to her five year old daughter who always called me names. I knew she couldn't do anything to me now. It was bad enough that the nuns called us bad, trash, and no good Crawfords, but to have this little girl calling me names all the time, I hated that. She was a cute girl, but she was really a spoiled brat. I did love her little sister. She was an adorable baby, and I would miss her.

When I finally got home to live with my brother and sister and our mom, they were living in Cincinnati in a second-floor apartment. It sure was different from the Ivy's' ten-room house where I had been living, but it was okay. It was just across the street from the little deli that our mom's new boyfriend owned and ran. Sometimes my brother and I would help him in the store and wait on the customers.

I got a job working at the corner drugstore, right up the street in the same block from the store near Findley Market. It was a busy area of town; they had a soda fountain, and we served lunches. We were allowed to eat whatever we wanted for free at lunch. I had never had a BLT sandwich before, and lunch was free to the workers, and the food was so good. I had one every time I worked, along with a chocolate milkshake. I thought I was in heaven. I enjoyed working there, and it really didn't matter that our mom took half of my paycheck, which was only seven dollars. She did the same with Joan and Floyd. It wasn't very much money—back then you didn't need as much—but it was a lot to me.

Then we moved to Newport, Kentucky, and lived in a second floor apartment. It was next to a house that we later found out was a place for prostitutes. When my brother found out, he was always in the bathroom watching the couples. He wouldn't let me go in, saying I was too young and a girl. In May, when Harry came home from the orphanage, he was introduced to the window in the bathroom to see the free "show". I thought what they were doing was awful, but they were boys. They always tried to hide it from me so I wouldn't tell. But I wouldn't have anyway, because I didn't want to get them in trouble.

The only thing I hated about that place was that I had to sleep in the same bed with our mom. She was like a total stranger to me, but I was small enough that I could sleep on the very edge of the bed so I would not touch her. It seemed so very wrong. I know now that part of it was because of what had happened to me in the orphanage. I got to the point where I did not like to be hugged anymore. It did not seem to be the thing to do back then anyway.

There were lots of times when my older sister, Joan, would take me roller-skating with her. She actually taught me to skate and even to waltz on roller skates. We wore real fancy short skirts.

At first I was embarrassed—I felt naked—but everyone else wore them so I got used to it. I enjoyed being with my big sister Joan, we had so much fun when we would go out together. Sometimes we would even just walk up and down Monmouth Street, the main street in Newport, checking out the shop windows. We loved looking at all the new clothes in the windows and dreaming of what we would like to have—shoes, dresses, all kinds of beautiful things. Joan, who had a good job, would often buy pretty dresses for our younger sisters, and we would take them to the orphanage when we would go to visit. When my sister Gerry was making her First Communion, Joan bought the material and I made her a dress. I also made a dress for Patty because she was going to lead the First Communion students down the aisle. I made Gerry's dress real sweet, and Patty's turned out to be too fancy. It was Gerry's special day, not Patty's. I felt bad about that. I don't know what I was thinking. Patty's dress was fluffy, and Gerry's dress was real sweet, just like she was and the dresses were perfect for them. They fit their personalities.

My older sister and I visiting our
younger sisters in the orphanage

In April of 1954 Joan got a boyfriend named Cletus and at first I got left behind a lot. I felt alone again. Cletus had a friend named Ron who used to go out with them. Cletus and Ron went to high school together. I was introduced to him and he was nice to me, so Joan took me along sometimes. We often went to Ross, Kentucky, and hung out where Ron's mother, Dot, worked in a restaurant. His grandmother Stella Renaker worked at the bar next door. At one time she had owned the bar where she was now working. Sometimes we ate in the bar and sometimes in the restaurant. The meals in both places were great. I would play the pinball machine for a nickel and I enjoyed it so much. Everyone had fun watching me get a kick out of the machine. It was like I was a kid again in a bar with men giving me nickels to play so they could watch me have fun. It was great and I loved it. Ron's mom liked me and she told Ron that I was a sweet girl.

One Friday in June, our mom came home from work, and she had all her bags packed. She was going on a vacation and she never said a word to Harry or me. Joan came home from work, and she was all packed too. She was going with our mom on the same vacation along with her boyfriend Cletus. No one told me about the vacation, or gave me any idea what I was supposed to do while they were gone. My brother Harry and I were just supposed to stay there all by ourselves, but I was scared. I couldn't believe our mom would do this to us. Floyd had since joined the navy and was away at boot camp. Our mom had no intention of leaving us anything to live on while she was gone. She was just going to go and leave us without a word. I guess she really didn't care about us after all. She also didn't care that her other six children were still in the orphanage and were being mistreated because she wouldn't pay. Yet she could take vacations without a care for any one of her children. That is how it was with our mom—go to work, go to the bar, come home, sleep, and go back to work. That is the way she lived her life.

So I cried and carried on and I was very upset that they were going to leave me home with my brother Harry. My sister Joan said she didn't have enough money to feed me, and our mom never offered a solution. Joan finally said I could go with them, but I had to ride in the backseat with their friend Ron. Our mom went in a different car with her boyfriend, Andy.

We had left Harry home alone because he had a job and had to work. I was worried about him but I knew he could take care of himself. He wasn't afraid to be at home alone but I was still worried, after all he had just gotten out of the orphanage.

So we went on vacation to Virginia Beach, Virginia. Our mom and Andy got one cabin and Cletus and Ron shared a cabin. Joan and I had our own cabin.

I just really loved the ocean. I thought it was fantastic and enormous. It was almost impossible to imagine that the Lord had made something so beautiful and wonderful for us to enjoy.

Somehow I managed to eat when they ate and had a good time. Ron was nice to me and he helped Joan to pay for my meals. So it worked out after all.

On the way home from the trip, I sat in the backseat again with Ron, and we started cuddling, something I had never experienced in my life. I was not even used to being hugged, so it was nice and no one seemed to care what we were doing. In the orphanage, I would have been punished for even a little bit of this kind of behavior. Even just holding hands with another girl was bad.

After that trip, Ron and I were friends, and we started going places with Cletus and Joan all the time. We continued to hang out at the restaurant where his mom worked. I was having more fun than I ever had in all my sixteen years of life. We were running around a lot, swimming at Martz Grove in Ross, and going to ballgames they had on the grounds. We went to movies and visited with Ron's Aunt Betty and Uncle Don who lived in Ross near Martz Grove. That summer was a lot of fun. I learned to catch the bus to Ross when Ron couldn't pick me up. It was a lot easier than riding a bus in Cincinnati.

I had at least ten aunts and uncles, lots of cousins, and nine brothers and sisters at this time, so Ron's family seemed small to me. Besides his mother and Grandma Stella, Aunt Betty, and Uncle Don, there was his Great-Aunt Marie and Uncle Charlie and his mom's Sister Ebo, who was married to a man named George. Aunt "Ebo" got that name because Ron couldn't say "Evelyn" when he was little, so he called her Aunt Ebo. Ron also had a Grandma and Grandpa Justice (his mom's dad and stepmom), but he never really ever saw them much. There was also a couple Ron called Aunt Chris and Uncle Jim, who were not really blood relatives. They were very good life-long friends of Ron's mom. Ron was an only child and didn't know his birthfather. His Grandma Stella had run Ron's dad off when he was just an infant so he never really knew his dad. What Ron lacked in family, he made up for in friends.

Ron had a cute four-year-old cousin named Buddy, who was a little monster. He would cry and carry on whenever we were going to a movie or the zoo or someplace like Coney Isle. His parents, Aunt Ebo and Uncle George, would always give in, and we would have to take him with us.

Ron told me his mother doted on Buddy more than she did him. He said she wasn't much of a mother to him at all. Ron's Aunt Ebo took care of Ron more than his mother did. Dot was always working or she went out and partied just like our mom did.

A couple of times, Ron would order me to do certain jobs around our house or he wouldn't take me out that night, so I obeyed. I thought I had to obey, because that's what I had been taught at the orphanage.

Sometime in August, Ron's Aunt Betty and her husband, Don, decided we were such a cute couple that we should get married. I was sixteen and Ron was eighteen. I guess it didn't matter that I was so young. I agreed because he told me he was going to die when he was twenty-one. I thought, *Oh good, I would have me some kids and no husband to deal with*, which is what I wanted. I didn't know what you did with a husband anyway yet. I didn't really know what you needed to do to make babies. I just thought you had to have a husband before you got a baby.

They told us we could go to Indiana to marry, because it was legal to marry in Indiana at age sixteen without parental permission. Uncle Don was a taxi driver and he said he would drive us.

Ron, Uncle Don and Aunt Betty planned everything and told me what I needed to do. I was to borrow a pretty dress from my sister, and they would pick me up at a certain time and drive us to Indiana to get married. So we were married on Monday August 24th, 1954. After we got back, I had to sneak the dress back into the house before Joan got home so she wouldn't know I borrowed it. We then went to Ross and had dinner and later that night I went back home to my house.

That Friday, the 28th, Ron planned that we would to tell our mom. We were at Pete's Place, which was a very popular bar in Melbourne. I went into the phone booth and called our mom. The phone in the booth was mounted to the wall and you had to talk into the mouthpiece while holding the other part of the phone up to your ear. I was telling our mom that I got married, and she just said, "Are you pregnant?" I didn't know what she meant. I didn't know what made you pregnant, so I couldn't imagine how or why I would be pregnant. We never did anything that I thought was bad yet. Well, I thought I was talking into the phone to her, but I was turned around talking to Ron and she couldn't hear me, and she hollered, "You are getting married in the church!" and hung up on me after saying she was coming to Pete's Place to get me. Well, I told Ron, and he grabbed me and we got in the car and drove a long way. We wound up in Lexington. He seemed to be afraid of our mother, but I never could figure out why or why we were running away. He hardly ever saw our mom because she was busy with her own life.

We stayed in Lexington and went to the movies all day. We watched the movie *Rear Window* at least four times, and then we went to a hotel. We drove back home on Sunday and met with our mom. First she bawled me out for running, because she said she had to drive down this really steep hill in the fog to meet with us. She said she practically had to walk the car all the way down the hill because of the fog. On Monday, she took us to my church to talk to the priest. He told us he would talk to us a few times, and if we still wanted to get married in the church, he would marry us. He told me to go to my house, and Ron was to stay at his home. That was the priest's rule, and that was fine with me. I don't think I realized that I had to live with Ron. I didn't know what was next anyway. My sister Joan wasn't married yet, so she never discussed things about sex and stuff like that with me. She got really mad at me because she said she wanted to set an example and be the first to get married. She'd never told me that she planned on getting married the following June, she also got really mad at me when she found out that I borrowed her best dress and wore it without her permission.

We waited and went to the priest and talked several times. About what, I don't remember—but it was probably about the church and its rules. It wasn't about what you had to do in a marriage with your spouse. One time he took us both aside and talked separately to each of us. He wanted to know if I really wanted to be married to this man. I was already too afraid of Ron to say no. I was afraid if I said no he would hurt me, I didn't know. I was just afraid of him already. He hadn't hit me. He was just very demanding.

The priest even said he would not tell Ron if I didn't want to marry him. He said he would just say he couldn't marry us because I was too young. But I was too afraid to say no. So Ron's mom and grandma planned a wedding. His grandma went and bought me a suit. It was a navy blue suit and it was ugly, but it was my "wedding dress".

They planned the wedding for the morning of September 18th, and a breakfast at our mom's afterward. Our mom picked up my grandparents and my brothers and sisters from the orphanage and brought them to the church. Our grandma had been very sick but our mom insisted that she come to the wedding since I was the first grandchild to get married. After the ceremony we went back to our mom's for breakfast. Ron's mom and grandma, Aunt Ebo, and the priest also came to the breakfast. Later that evening we went to a small reception at Ron's home. His Grandma Stella and two aunts and some of my aunts, uncles and cousins also came to the reception.

Later that night I finally realized what couples did when they got married. I didn't like it. To me, it was disgusting, and I thought it was bad. But I was told that it was my duty as a wife so I complied. We were happy most of the time and things were good.

In January, my grandma who had been really sick for quite a while went to the doctor one day. While she was in the doctor's office, she had a heart attack and died right there. They could not find my grandpa anywhere. They knew he had taken her to the doctor, but they did not realize that he was sitting in his car waiting for her. When one of the aunts went to the doctor's office, there he was sitting in his car. That was so sad. Our grandma was a wonderful woman. She was always so good to us and made us feel loved. She never wanted us to go into the orphanage.

Our wedding day with my grandparents in 1954

Chapter 5

After the wedding, we had moved in with Ron's mother and grandmother in Ross. His mother had a boyfriend who ran a butcher shop in the basement of our apartment building. I would be home in the day while Ron worked. One day while I was ironing, he came by and said hi. The next thing I knew, he was grabbing me from behind. This frightened me because I could not stand anyone grabbing me from behind, not even my husband. I always fought Ron when he did that, and I was able to fight Charlie off too. He told me he would show me how a man was supposed to treat a woman and I wanted no part of it. He finally left me alone. It was bad enough I had to do what my husband wanted me to do. Since I was married in the church, Ron always reminded that I had to obey my husband. He would say the bible says, "Woman, be subject to your husband."

We lived in the apartment for about another six months, and I finally talked Ron into moving to Covington, Kentucky, which was closer to my family. That lasted for three months. He did not like Covington at all, or me being close to my family. Then his mother bought an old house that needed a lot of work, on a nice little piece of property. We bought a little mobile home, twenty-nine feet long by eight feet wide, and parked it on his mom's property. Ron would always tell me that I was too stupid to get a job, so I went and got me a job working at Pogue's department store in downtown Cincinnati as a wrapper. I really liked that job. I would catch the bus to work and back home and since it was in downtown Cincinnati, catching the bus to that area was easy. After about six months I quit that job.

Uncle George and Aunt Ebo were pregnant with their second child. They took Buddy and moved out of the little cottage they were living in and into the second floor of the house Ron's mom was having remodeled. Uncle George and Aunt Ebo only had two rooms up there on the second floor, and they would cook and eat downstairs with Dot. She wanted them close by.

In the meantime, our mother was pregnant at the age of thirty-nine with her eleventh child. I wanted a baby so bad and yet she was the one who got pregnant. It wasn't fair; I had been married for two years and still didn't have a baby. She didn't need a baby because I still had brothers and sisters in the orphanage that she wasn't taking care of. It was a good thing our grandmother had passed away; she would have been more heartbroken.

Our mom decided that she and Andy had to get married. After they got married, the trustees of the orphanage made her take my sisters and brothers home from the orphanage. (The orphanage was closed and torn down four years later.) I felt so bad for my younger siblings when they came home. They had it worse than we (older ones) did before we went into the orphanage. We older kids we were used to not having anything before we went to the orphanage; living in three rooms, finding our food wherever we could, and sleeping on floors on piles of clothes. These poor kids were used to sleeping in nice beds and having plenty of food to eat. Yes, at the orphanage, some of the nuns weren't the kindest to the children and you had to obey the rules, but that was nothing compared to what my younger siblings went home to. They had three rooms and a toilet and no tub to bathe in. There was no hot water so they had to heat water, and fill a metal tub to bathe in. (The tub would be put in the kitchen when they wanted a bath.)

They were used to better living conditions, so it was very hard on them. The boys had two beds to sleep in, (bunk beds) and the girls slept wherever they could. Naturally, our mom and her new husband had their own double bed.

The younger kids went to a parochial grade school after they left the orphanage. The other children at the school and even some of the nuns who taught there treated them badly, just like they did at the orphanage. This was probably because once again our mom did not pay their way, so the nuns took it out on the kids.

I did not get to visit my family very often, because Ron really didn't like how they lived, he was good to them most of the time but he didn't want me around them. For some reason he was always really mean to my little brother Frank. Ron was always making Frank work and clean things up. There were four girls, two boys, and a baby who lived there too, but he would only pick on my younger brother Frank just like they did at the orphanage. There wasn't much food in the fridge, but there were plenty of roaches and ketchup. Through all of this our mom was always dressed great and wore plenty of makeup and jewelry. She always seemed to be having fun.

Our brother Floyd would come home on leave from the navy to visit. When he was home, there were nine people including our mom and step-dad trying to live in a three-room house, with one bathroom, no tub, and not enough food for all of them to eat.

My younger sister had taught the boys to steal stuff so that they could eat—even potato chips, candy, and junk food. They stole only what she asked them to. There was never any older adult supervision, like at the orphanage. She also sent them to the store to steal clothing they needed, especially underwear and socks. She showed the girls how to put the underwear on and walk out. One day the store Security followed them and said she had been watching them. The girls explained that they needed some underclothes. The lady told them that she would let them go this time, but not to do it again. They were afraid so they listened and never did it again.

My two younger brothers also got caught stealing one day at a store by the owner. The owner had a really nice talk with them and encouraged them to stay in school. He also offered one of them a job. He told the storeowner that he wouldn't steal again but he didn't want to work at that store. My brother got a job working in a garage and the owner of the garage was very good to him.

My brother Ron decided that he was going to finish high school and he even helped our little sister Gerry, so that she could finish school. They both graduated from Holmes High in Covington and we were all very proud of them. They were the only ones out of the ten of us to finish high school.

Of course, our mom was never at home. She went to work, and after work, she went to the bar. She would come home to sleep and go back to work again. She was married to Andy, her second husband, at this time, but he didn't come home either. Andy would give Beverly, our sister, some money to buy food, but it wasn't enough for all the kids. Sometimes Beverly would take money out of his wallet for food.

Our mom only cooked a nice meal on Sunday. During the week, my sisters took care of our baby sister Sandy. I tried to convince our mom to give the baby to me. After all, she already had ten kids she could not take care of, but she wouldn't. Our other sister Joan, who was married by this time, also wanted to take Sandy. Our mom had the other kids to watch the baby, so she would not let us have Sandy. At least she was working.

Christmas with Ron's Mom and Step-dad in 1956

Ron's mother, Dot, married a fantastic guy named Jim. Jim was someone she had gone to school with, and she had met again at my sister Joan's wedding. I was in Joan's wedding and so was Jim's daughter Ella Marie. Dot had a ball with Jim that night. They started to go out all the time and eventually got married. They had a rough beginning because she was very controlling. Every time they had a fight, Jim would pack his things in a pillowcase and leave, but he always came back. During this time Jim was helping Uncle George finish the remodeling on Dot's home. One day after they put the new doors in, Jim said, "I am not leaving again, because the doors won't fit in a pillowcase." After that, things settled down and Jim and Dot got along just fine.

There were a lot of times Ron and I would walk down to Martz Grove and go swimming with Dot and Jim. We had a lot of fun with them. Dot would tell us stories of how she and Aunt Chris would have parties at the pool at night and go swimming in the nude—I thought that was crazy. But I guess they had fun. I wasn't afraid of Ron when Jim was around. One day I was sitting on the side of the pool and Jim came along and playfully pushed me in the deep end. I heard Ron holler, "Hey, she can't swim," but he didn't jump in to help me. Jim jumped in and when he did he skinned the whole side of his thigh. Ron just sat there and laughed at me. He told me I had no business sitting on the side of the pool at the deep end if I couldn't swim. Jim felt bad for pushing me in but he hollered at Ron for not going in after me. Jim was a great stepfather-in-law and a lot of fun to be around. He was good to me and did not like the way Ron treated me.

Ron would smack me around, pull my hair, and dare me to tell anyone or say a word to anyone, especially his mom. Ron called me names all the time. I was always a whore, just like our mom, or I was a slut and nobody else would ever want me. I was used to being called names, but I thought he was supposed to love me.

Once again Ron started telling me that I was stupid and too dumb to even try to go to work. So eventually I went and got another job. I enjoyed working, and everyone treated me very nice. I was not used to that and it felt good to be treated nice. Ron was always giving me orders to keep my mouth shut and not tell anyone at work how he treated me. I was so afraid of him that I obeyed. There were times we would be riding along in the car and he would start hitting me and screaming at me. I often wished the people in the other cars would see him and blow their horn at him and make him stop, but that never happened.

When I worked, Ron would take my pay and give me just enough for lunch and bus fare. We lived in the mobile home then, and the bus stop was over a block from home. I always walked home from the bus stop, even in the rain and snow. Ron had a lot of friends that he hung out with and if they called and needed a ride, he would jump up and pick them up right away. A few of them would even ask him why he couldn't pick me up when the weather was bad, and all he would say was that "she could walk."

Ron spent a lot of time with his friends during the week and even on weekends. That was until he got a girlfriend. Ron was working at the funeral home at the time, and I found a letter from his girlfriend. He took a swing at me for reading the letter and said it was not meant for me. I ducked and his fist went through the cupboard door. He got so mad at me because I ducked. (I don't know how he explained the hole in the door to his boss.)

There were times when Ron would say he had to go somewhere and he would take me to visit my family. I was happy to get to visit my family but I later realized that this was probably when he was meeting up with a girlfriend.

One Saturday in June Ron told me that he had to have a ring resized for me but he didn't tell me where he was going and he dropped me off to visit my family. I didn't know what ring he was talking about because I never even saw this ring. Our mom was at the bar so I walked up to see her with my sister Shirley. While I was at the bar one of my brothers called to tell me that they heard on the radio that my mobile home was on fire. Our mom drove me back to Ross to see what had happened. I was devastated and I screamed and cried. Dot held me while I cried. Our mom was there, but it was my mother-in-law who held me until I stopped crying.

Dot asked me where Ron was, but I didn't know so my father-in-law Jim went looking for him. I don't know how Jim found him, but Ron came back home with him. My father-in-law told me Ron was on a picnic with his girlfriend who lived in Cincinnati. I found out later that that was the day he gave that girl the engagement ring that he said was for me.

The mobile home was destroyed, and we lost everything. The thing I hated most to lose was my bride doll that I had won in the orphanage. It was the prettiest thing I ever owned as a child that was all mine.

All we had left was the clothes we had on our backs and I had to wear those same clothes to work that Monday, because the stores were not open on Sundays. I had on heels and I had to wait until lunchtime to get a pair of flat shoes to wear at work.

The mobile home had a wiring defect that caused the fire. I worked for an insurance company, and one of our agents wanted us to sue the company we got it from because they had sold many bad mobile homes in the past. But Ron said to forget it, so we got a very used twenty-nine-foot mobile home. It was small and not new like the other one, but it was ours.

I hated gas stoves, and that was what was in the mobile home. One Saturday I went to light the oven, and *bam*, it exploded. It blew me back across the room and knocked me into the wall. Ron was lying on the couch, and he just busted out laughing. He didn't bother to jump up and ask if I was okay or anything. I was sore from hitting the wall, but I was furious at him for laughing at me. I swore that I would never light a gas stove again and Ron had to light the stove after that if he wanted me to cook.

Sometimes, when Ron was working at the funeral home, he would take me with him to work. He allowed me to go to the movie theater, which was only two blocks away from his work.

I would walk to the theater and then walk back when the movie was over. I was always given strict orders to be back at exactly ten o'clock, but I did not realize that meant that I had to leave the theater whether the movie was over or not. If I wasn't there when he got off work at ten o'clock, he said he would go home without me and he did. Mr. Dobbling, the owner of the funeral home, would call him up and tell him to come and get me. Ron told him, "She shouldn't have been late, let her find her own way home, she knows how to walk." It was more than six miles to our home. After calling Ron several times, Mr. Dobbling gave up, and he sent me home in a taxi. When I got home, I got a thorough beating. Ron would say, "This will teach you not to be late and who the boss is." After this happened several times, I quit going to the movies. I was tired of being hit and not being able to watch the whole movie. He couldn't even wait ten minutes for me.

Some weekends we would have to spend all night at the funeral home where Ron worked. I hated this because it was a funeral home, and that in it's self was scary to me. But mostly I hated it because Ron would make me sleep closest to the door. When I knew there was a body there for a service, it really freaked me out. Sleeping near the door reminded me of the door I slept next to at the orphanage. I was always scared when I forced to sleep by the big heavy metal door that would moan and groan, especially when there was a storm or when the wind was blowing really hard. This is why I was so afraid at the funeral home. I used to think Ron was scared too but then I would think that he was too mean to be afraid of anything.

We were married for three years and I wondered why I wasn't pregnant yet. Once I went to the doctor and asked why I wasn't having any luck getting pregnant. He told me to just "relax and you will get pregnant." Ron's grandma also told me not to worry and she also told me "once you get that baby machine working you can't stop it".

Finally we were expecting our first baby around the first of March. I had an easy pregnancy and the only time I thought I might be sick was when I would fix bacon. The smell of the bacon made me nauseous but of course, Ron had to have a pound of bacon on weekends and half a dozen eggs for breakfast. He was a big eater, and it had to be perfect or I had to fix it over.

I was working in an office at this time typing letters from a Dictaphone. I couldn't type very fast but I knew how to do the "hunt and peck" system. My boss was a nice guy and he knew I wanted the job so he was patient. I was good at filing and other things around the office, and I thoroughly enjoyed the work and the people I worked with. I knew that I would have to leave when I was seven months pregnant. The funny thing was that all the other girls who worked this position before me also left because of a pregnancy. I hated to leave; they were all so good to me and treated me well. They actually babied me because I was the youngest one there. They were all older and never married or had kids. I was always so happy when I was at work. I had nothing to be afraid of.

When it was time for me to leave, they celebrated my leaving by taking me to lunch and showering me with a great big gift box. It was filled with lots of necessary baby items and little things a baby needed. It had matching gowns, sleepers, blankets, diapers, pins, lotions, bibs, and sleepers. Everything was so beautiful, and it was all in white, mint green, and yellow. We never knew if it was a boy or a girl, so those were the perfect colors and also my favorite colors. It was really great. The big boss even sent a gift. He gave me a beautiful white shawl and a mint green sweater set. There was so much stuff that I had to call Ron to pick me up. I couldn't possibly get it all home on the bus.

During that time, I used to baby-sit for my friend Janet and her husband Jack, who lived across the street up on a hill. I enjoyed watching her boys who were babies at the time because they were good babies. I remember when they came home her husband would drive me home because he knew I would be scared walking down the hill in the dark. I never gave Ron any of the money I made for the babysitting.

Ron's Grandma, mom and step-dad were happy that we were having a baby. Dot had a baby shower for us and we received more lovely things we needed for our new little one. My sister Joan already had a little girl named Theresa, and was expecting her second baby. She never talked about her pregnancy; it was something you didn't discuss back then. I did ask her how the baby got out, and she just said there is a special place down there. It would have been embarrassing to read books on it, but Ron wouldn't let me read them anyway. I wasn't sure what to expect, but one morning I got up to go to the bathroom and when I went to get back into bed, a gush of water suddenly let loose. At first I got scared because I thought I had peed on the floor. Ron said, "No, your water just broke." All of a sudden, I was having a lot of pain so we called the doctor, and we went to the hospital. Back then the doctors sedated you but you would wake up with each pain. Ron would come into the room and I would scream and yell at him that he was never to touch me again. No one told me that it would hurt. Joan always said, "Just wait, you'll see," when I asked her about having a baby.

The pain was forgotten as soon as I saw my beautiful nine-pound-four-ounce baby boy. I had wanted to name him James Ronald, but my sister who had her second baby in December named her son James. So I chose Ronald James. He was beautiful, and I enjoyed him. He was born on March the 14th, 1958.

Ronald James or "Ronnie" as we called him was baptized at our parish church in Melbourne. I wanted my brother Harry to be his godfather, but he was in a TB sanitarium. (Harry was eighteen years old when he was diagnosed with tuberculosis (TB). He was sent to a sanitarium and quarantined for almost three years.) So Ron's friend stood in as a proxy godfather for my brother Harry and Ron's mom was his godmother.

When Harry left the sanitarium he went to live with our grandpa because the living conditions were better. I was happy Harry was able to come to Ronnie's 1st Birthday party.

Ron's grandma liked to buy Ronnie outfits and one time she bought him a little girl's outfit. I don't know what she was thinking. Ron told me I had to put it on him so she could see him in it. I did, but as soon as we got back home, I packed it away in case someday we had a little girl. Ronnie was a good little boy and he did all the things he was supposed to do, right on time. He even walked at nine months.

We celebrated Christmas in that little twenty-nine-by-eight-foot mobile home, and there was just not enough room for the baby and all his presents. So we went and bought a forty-foot trailer that was twelve feet wide, and that was much better. We had lots of room now.

Our mom and some of my sisters and brothers would come to visit us. My baby sister Sandy would play with Ronnie and Michael, Ron's cousin, who was almost the same age as Sandy. Ron had poured us a nice size patio with the help of his Uncle George and some friends. It was a really nice place to gather in the summer.

Ron still worked at the funeral home and sometimes we would go and have dinner at Wells Tavern in Ross, where Ron's mom used to work. The man who owned the bar, Oscar, was always teasing Ron about who was going to be his first "customer" from Ross. Surely enough, Oscar was the first "customer" from Ross. Shortly after that Ron quit the Funeral and had several low paying jobs.

When Ronnie was six months old, I was sitting in the living room rocking him to sleep and the most awful thing happened. Ron's cousin Buddy had gotten off the school bus, and asked his mom, if he could cross the street to visit his friend. Ebo was standing there holding her two-year-old son Michael and she said it was okay. Buddy bolted across the highway without looking and a passing car hit him. The driver of the car didn't see him until it was too late, and he flew about fifty feet in the air and hit a telephone pole. I watched in shock as he landed right on the road in front of our mobile home. It was awful. We called Ron at work; he was now working at a concrete company with his Uncle George. Ron told his Uncle George, who was Buddy's dad, what happened and they were both home in about five minutes. Buddy was only seven years old, and he was killed instantly.

We all knew the driver of the car that hit Buddy and he was devastated. We were all very shook up. I was crying when Ron got home and he hollered at me told me to stop crying. He said that I didn't like Buddy anyway, and he didn't see why I was crying. Buddy was an innocent child and I did love him. It was a very sad time for all of us. I was holding my baby and rocking him, and I saw it happen.

The funeral was held at Dobbling Funeral Home in Fort Thomas, where Ron used to work. Mrs. Dobbling and her family lived upstairs, so she watched Ronnie for us during the funeral. She enjoyed spending time with Ronnie. Her children were all grown and she didn't have any grandchildren yet. The Dobblings had just recently lost a son in a car accident on the eve of their daughter's wedding. It was a horrible accident, and it was very hard on them.

Soon after that, I got myself another job. I was tired of being called lazy and no good again. I went to work at a place called Signs of the Times Publishing Co. on Walnut Street in Cincinnati. I liked working there, but I had to take Ronnie with me. I would catch the bus and my sister Beverly would meet me at work and take Ronnie. In the morning, she would walk up "Sycamore Hill" carrying Ronnie and the diaper bag. In the evening, her friend would drive them back down to my place of work. It was hard dragging Ronnie to the bus terminal everyday and getting on the bus with him, but it was good to be able to spend the extra time with him.

Sometimes when we would get off the bus in Ross, it would be raining hard or even snowing. I would ask Ron to pick me up at the bus stop because I had the baby and the diaper bag to carry. It was a little more than a block to walk home and he didn't care. He only cared about himself and he didn't want to be disturbed.

If it was one his young friends, he would go right away. They didn't even have to wait.

I cooked supper, took care of the baby, did the housework and laundry, and always did what I was told. I couldn't drive a car because he didn't want to teach me and I never really wanted to learn. I just did as I was told. Besides, I hated cars—he always drove crazy to scare me, going too fast or slamming on the brakes. Sometimes he would turn off the engine and coast down a very steep hill. When the floodwaters were up, he would drive right through them. I was so afraid the car would float away because I couldn't swim, and he thought it was funny. I would cry and tell him to stop. We always had the baby in the car, but he never cared.

Ron did let me run around with my sister Beverly and her friend Lorraine. I always thought it was because she was a former nun and Ron figured that I was safe from men being around her. Ron always called her a "lessie". I never knew exactly what that meant at the time. I know now it means that she liked women, not men, and he thought I was safe around her.

When John F. Kennedy was running for president, I was allowed to campaign for him, with Beverly and Lorraine. Ron and I were crazy about Kennedy, as was the whole country. We helped at the different campaign headquarters. Mr. Kennedy came to Cincinnati, so we went to Fountain Square to hear him talk. We hoped we could get close to him and we would up standing right in front of him. Beverly was holding Ronnie on her shoulders and John F. Kennedy reached down to shake hands with the people. Beverly actually got to shake his hand and it was fantastic. We were so excited. I actually got to touch his sleeve as he was shaking her hand and then he turned away to leave. It was great to be that close to an incoming president, especially John F. Kennedy.

Shortly after that, my sister Beverly moved to Delaware with her friend Lorraine, so I had to find a new sitter. Our mother had already told me when I got pregnant that she would not watch my kids, like I would even want her to. I got my younger sister Patty to watch Ronnie over the summer. She was fifteen years old and she would take him to Martz Grove, when the weather was nice. Ron's mom was constantly telling me that Patty was only taking Ronnie to the park so she could flirt with the young boys. Ronnie was fine and happy, and at least she watched him for me, which was more than Ron's mom would do for us. My sister was a teenager, and she never did half of the things that my mother-in-law had done as a young person.

Chapter 6

Ron started managing a softball team and had lots of new friends. We went wherever there was a game and I had to go with him. I came to realize he was terribly jealous of everyone who looked at me. He wanted me right by his side. I don't know why, though, because he always said I was fat (at 120 pounds) and ugly, so why was he worried?

There was a guy on the team who took a liking to me, and Ron was so jealous. Ron would always say "just wait you're going to get what-for" (which meant a beating) when we get home just because I was talking to him. He was a nice guy and very handsome, but I wasn't allowed to talk to him. If Ron caught me anywhere near this guy, he would get furious. I was married and had a baby so I didn't care about the guy, but he was nice to me. So yeah, I spoke with him, and I was always in trouble when I got home. I would take a beating and be called every name in the book, like a bitch, a whore and a slut.

There were times when Ron was angry about something and he would kick me out of bed and tell me I had to wash the walls down, or do some work that he thought I didn't do the right way in the first place. Sometimes when he would come home from work, he would put on white gloves and run around and check over the top of the doors just to make sure I dusted everything just right. He was odd. He always told me I was always no good, just like our mom. That was his favorite thing to say, and that no one else would ever want me. He also told me he did me a favor by marrying me.

One weekend I left Ron. I took Ronnie and a few of our things and I caught a bus to my grandpa's house. Our mom and my brothers and sisters were now living with my grandpa. Grandpa let our mom move in with him after her second husband left her after about four years of marriage. I was only there for two days, and Ron brought some of my things over. He said he tore up our marriage license and threw it out because he didn't need it anymore. The very next day, someone was fixing bacon and I got nauseous. I got to thinking about it and sure enough, I was pregnant. I thought I had no other way out, so I went back to Ron.

It didn't get any better. Ron would beat me and then say he was sorry and then do it again and again. It didn't matter that I was pregnant. He would punch me in the stomach and then started telling me that it was not his baby. I naturally knew better, and I also knew that he did too. I couldn't stand sex anyway, so why would I do that with someone else? He was crazy to think it could be anyone else's baby, because I was never out of his sight, except for the weekend that I left him. I didn't know anyone in Covington, and I wasn't gone long enough to meet someone.

One time, Shirley and I went to the bar to find our mom to visit with her. When Ron found out, he was furious with me, but more so at Shirley. He quit speaking to Shirley for several years. He said it was all her fault that I was in a bar, but I was four years older than her. Then again I got "what-for" when I got home.

He continued to beat me and put me down, always hitting me in the stomach. I was so afraid for the baby. I would pray for God to please make my baby be okay, and help me to know what I was doing wrong for these things to be happening. I didn't know what to do I told my mom, and she just said, "You married him, you live with it," or "You made your bed, now lie in it." It was probably what someone had told her. All I worried about was, what did I do to get him upset? When he said jump, I jumped. I did everything I was told almost immediately. I obeyed him like I was a kid in the orphanage again. I thought it was my job to obey my husband, or so I was told. I wasn't even allowed to drink "his" soft drinks. If we had to go get a loan to borrow money and they would ask a lot of questions, he would kick me under the desk so I would keep my mouth shut. I obeyed.

Ron hardly ever let me go to church or even confession like you were supposed to. I guess he was afraid I would say something to the priest about him. He never let me do anything by myself. He was either jealous or afraid, and he couldn't have that.

It came to a point when all of the sudden, we couldn't pay our bills anymore. I never really spent any money, so it wasn't my fault. Ron handled all the bills and he was the one who went to the store for most everything we needed. When I worked, he took most of my money and gave me exactly what he wanted me to have and nothing else.

Ron spoke to his mom, and she said she would help. She said that we could move in with her in the two empty rooms she had upstairs. Ron's Aunt Ebo and Uncle George had lived with her in those rooms but moved out after their son Buddy was killed. They bought themselves a mobile home near where George worked in Melbourne.

We stored our furniture in one room and slept with Ronnie in the other room. We all shared the downstairs kitchen and living room. There were three bedrooms on the first floor. Dot and Jim shared one bedroom and Ron's Grandma Stella slept in one. The other bedroom was for company that stayed on weekends.

I learned to cook a lot more different things living there with them. Dot totally managed all of our money and paid off all the bills that we owed in due time. Jim also had a married daughter with two children who needed their help, and there was no room for them in the house. So he would help them through the hard times.

Soon after we moved in, Ron's grandma was diagnosed with a blood disease called leukemia. They didn't give her much time to live. This was in January, I was five months pregnant at the time and Ronnie was going to be two in March. When he heard his great-grandma was sick, he pulled up his little rocking chair by her bed and said he was going to watch after her.

On May 1st I was washing all the baby clothes I had saved from Ronnie. I was getting them ready because my due date was May 5th. Grandma Stella passed away the following day on May 2nd. Luckily, this time Ron was not working at the funeral home.

Ron was still working at the concrete place where his Uncle George worked. He had worked a lot of low-paying jobs, after he left the funeral home, and now he finally got a good-paying job in an office he liked.

Ron was still mean to me, but not as often, because his parents were always home. Ron's stepdad Jim didn't like the way he treated me. I usually only got hollered at when we went up to bed. He would still get very angry and hit on me when they weren't home. When they were home he would dared me to cry for fear that they would hear me. Somehow he knew all the tricks.

In the middle of May, Jim was working on the backyard getting it ready for the summer parties. He was always ordering loads of dirt to fill in low spots and asked me to help him shovel. Since the baby was late, he said that all the shoveling would help get the baby out sooner. Beside he couldn't get anyone else to do it, and I was a good worker, so I helped him.

A couple of times he tried to give me castor oil (to get me to go into labor), but I couldn't get it past my nose; it was the most nasty, awful-smelling stuff I ever tasted. Since that didn't work, he would get me outside in the backyard to start shoveling the dirt again. I didn't care, I was always helping with something, and he was a very nice father-in-law.

Ron's Aunt Chris and Uncle Jim would always come to visit on weekends and they would stay in the extra bedroom. We would all play cards until late into the night. They drank a lot and smoked too much—I hated the smoke -but I enjoyed playing cards. They were good company and very good friends to my son and me. We lived out in the "country" and Ron didn't want me out of his sight, so this was a fun thing to do.

When I was pregnant with my first baby, Ron's stepdad, Jim, bet me a bottle of wine what the baby would be, a boy or girl. He called for a girl and I called for a boy, and I won. I loved a certain Mogen David wine even though Ron would forbid me to drink. Jim never cared. He still bet me anyway and I would have a small drink once in a while. With our second child, it was the same bet. I still bet on a boy and he chose a girl, and I won again. I wanted another boy so Ronnie would have a brother. I guess they wanted me to have a girl since there were so many boys in the family. We already had a boy and Jim's first grandchild from his daughter was a boy, and Ron's Aunt Ebo had two boys.

On the morning of May 15th, 1960, almost two weeks after my due date, I finally went into labor, and late that evening my second beautiful little boy was born. I wanted a smaller baby this time, and he weighed nine pounds three ounces, which was only one ounce smaller than Ronnie. They were both big babies. I checked him all over, and he was perfect, ten fingers and ten toes. He had a very chubby-face and fuzzy blond hair and we named him Kenneth Allen. Allen was for his great-grandpa. (What Ron didn't know was that I named him after the guy's brother, who was always nice to me at the ball games. So for once I out foxed him and never ever told anyone, until now.) Kenny was adorable, and I won the bottle of wine again. Jim had fun betting with me, and he knew how Ron treated me and didn't like it. Jim and I got along well. This was one of my first experiences in finding out that there were some decent men in this world. (I knew priests were nice, but I didn't look at them as men.)

After Kenny was born, we still lived with Ron's parents, so we also had Kenny baptized at the same parish church in Melbourne, My sister Shirley and her husband Jim were godparents to Kenny. We actually named him Kenneth Allen, but the priest put Kenneth

Joseph (he had to have a saint's name) on his baptismal record. I really enjoyed living with Dot and Jim. It was kind of a fun time for me because I always had company. Not help—I didn't need it, I always took complete care of my babies, and I loved it. They were mine, and I wasn't too keen on someone else watching them for me.

Ron still continued to say that Kenny was not his child. He was harder on Kenny, even though he looked more like him than our son Ronnie.

Sometimes the boys would get a paddleball for a gift, like at Easter. After the ball broke off, I would save them for a little threat if they were bad. These were babies, and I thought they were supposed to be perfect like they expected us to be in the orphanage. My mother-in-law would hide them on me so I wouldn't get after them. I would always the find paddleballs behind the refrigerator. Dot never said anything to Ron when he got after the boys.

Well it took forever to get our bills paid, and we were still living with Dot and Jim a year later. Then I got pregnant again, so we spent another eleven months at Dot's. I didn't care because I enjoyed living there. I learned to cook better, and I didn't get beat as much. Ron mostly pulled my hair when he didn't want to yell at me when they were at home.

The morning our third baby was born, July 23rd, 1961 I was up at four o'clock in the morning. I was real restless and couldn't sleep. Kenny, who was fourteen months old at the time, was already awake. He couldn't sleep either. I didn't want him to wake anyone up so we went down to the basement. While he played, I did some ironing. I heard a big boom and went running. Kenny had picked up a soft-drink bottle, and somehow it blew up in his hand and cut his little hand really bad. So I got his dad up to drive us to the hospital, since I still could not drive. When we got to the hospital, they strapped him down on the bed with a pillow on his tummy. They had to keep him still to stitch the cut on his hand. He screamed his head off the whole time. You would have thought that they were killing him. It was very upsetting to see what they were doing to my baby, but I knew it had to be done. It was difficult for me to watch and listen to him scream. After that incident, every time we saw someone in any kind of a uniform, the milkman, mailman, doctors or nurses, he would start screaming. It must have really scared him bad.

While we were there, they noticed that I was having labor pains. They asked me how far apart the pains were, and then they made me stay. Ron took Kenny home to his mom and came back to the hospital to be with me. We had our first baby girl on July 23rd, 1961. She weighed seven pounds three ounces and she looked very tiny and frail. She was so little compared to the boys, but she was beautiful, and she was my Dorothy. I had an Aunt Dorothy who I was very fond of, and I loved her and her name. My mother-in-law was also named Dorothy so Ron allowed me to give her that name. I was very happy he agreed with me.

Chapter 7

When Dorothy was six weeks old, we finally got to move out of Dot's home. Dot was very upset because she didn't want us to move out. She was going to miss us all. She even liked me, which seemed strange to me. I wasn't sure too many people did.

We moved to Highland Heights, and lived in a small house. It was perfect, and I enjoyed living there. I was allowed to go to church when Ron would to take me. I had to take all three children with me and sit in the "cry room." They weren't too bad, just a little hard to handle all alone. Once in a while, someone would offer to hold one of the kids for me. Dorothy was a newborn, Ronnie was three years old, and Kenny was fourteen months. I literally had my hands full, but I was happy with my children. I took them for a lot of walks in the afternoon, just to get out and to keep the house clean for a little bit longer. The house had to be perfect when Ron got home, plus, his supper had to be ready when he walked in the door.

We only stayed in Highland Heights for about six months, and then I got pregnant again. There wasn't enough room for another baby at that house, so we moved to Crescent Springs. As usual, I set about packing everything up while taking care of the babies.

Ron never lifted a finger to help with anything. He wouldn't even hold one of the babies; he would always say it wasn't his job. I got things packed up, and he and his friends moved the big stuff like the stove and refrigerator and other heavy stuff. I did have some help from one of my sisters to watch over the babies.

Ron gave the orders and I obeyed and got things done. I kept the house clean and neat and I also cut the grass. I also learned to fix anything that went out of whack. I was always happy with my babies and I took very good care of them, even though they kept me up a lot at night. I couldn't let them cry because Ron would kick me and make me get up and "shut them up." I thought that was the way it was supposed to be, so I complied.

One night a week, which was payday, he would bring food home from McDonald's for the kids and me. He would bring Frisch's for himself—two Big Boys, a fish sandwich, an order of onion rings, and some fries. This was fine with me because I didn't have to cook.

Ron did a lot of sleeping when he was home. He would come home from work, eat then lie on the couch, and watch TV. I had to keep the kids quiet for him. If he couldn't hear the TV, he would scream, "Shut them kids up!" If anyone walked in front of the TV, he would yell again. Even after I thought he was asleep, he would still holler at any noise.

Ron's mom would call crying all the time, saying how much she missed us, especially the kids. She wanted us to visit every week, and Ron never wanted to go. (She would never come to visit us). When we would go to visit, Ron would just lay up stairs on the couch all day, sleeping and watching sports on TV. Dot, Jim and the rest of us would be outside having fun with the kids until it was time to eat. I would have to beg and plead with Ron to get him to take us to Ross. I needed a break and I needed someone to talk to besides the little ones. After sucking up to him and that was hard to do, I could get him to agree to go. I just wanted to go somewhere with the kids instead of staying home all the time. The kids had a great time at Grandma's house, and she always cooked us a really good meal. After a while Ron was willing to go because that would count as one of our meals for the week and that helped to stretch our money.

In March when it was Ronnie's birthday, we would go to Ross to celebrate. Because it was spring, the river was always up and Route 8 would be flooded and closed to traffic. We would drive part of the way down Upper 8 Mile Road and park the car. We would walk from there, over the hill, carrying the birthday cake and three little kids. It was quite a trek. The kids enjoyed the trip to Grandma's but leaving Grandma's was much harder; it was more uphill than down, and they were all tired. But they survived it. We were always walking anyway. I was always taking the babies on long walks. It gave me a break from watching them in the house for a while, and it gave them something different to do.

I enjoyed living in Crescent Springs. The church was only about three blocks away, and I could walk. Ron never wanted me to go to church, and if I did, I had to take all the kids, which is what I did when I had the chance. I loved going to church because it was peaceful, and I could talk to Jesus and no one would know what I said to him. He wouldn't tell on me.

In our backyard in Crescent Springs, there were lots of blackberry bushes. The kids and I would pick the berries and wash them up real good. When Ron got home he would actually make blackberry jam. I was amazed that he knew how to make blackberry jam and also that he wanted to do it for us. That was one good thing that he did do for us.

At Easter time, we had gotten the kids two chickens and a duck. The chickens were so messy, and as soon as they got big enough we gave them away. There was a family down the street who had a lot of children, and we gave the chickens to their kids. They wound up fixing them for a meal. Their oldest boy, called Bozo, was a good friend of ours by now. When Ron wasn't sleeping, he would be out in the side yard, playing football and baseball with Bozo and other teenagers in the neighborhood.

We decided to let Bozo watch our duck when it was time for the baby's birth. When we got home from the hospital with the baby, he told us his family had a great meal out of the duck. I was okay with that because the Duck was so nasty.

On September 5th, 1962 we had our second baby girl, named Barbara Marie. She was beautiful, all eight pounds four ounces of her. She was our first baby to have a head-full of coal-black hair. The nurses at the hospital pulled it on top of her head and tied a pink ribbon around it. It was just enough to make a curl on top. She looked perfect. All my other babies were beautiful fuzzy-haired blondes. (I won the bottle of wine again from Jim.) I came home from the hospital with our baby to a fourteen-month-old, a two-year-old, and a four-year-old. It was great with all these babies and they all took their naps around the same time. I always had two that were in diapers and since I only had two-dozen cloth diapers, I was always washing diapers. We had a wringer washer and no dryer, and everything had to be hung outside, which was fine with me. I loved it when the diapers froze on the line along with the towels and other clothes, because they felt softer when they thawed out. I didn't really care; it was what I was used to anyway. When Ron did get me a used dryer from his stepdad, I was only allowed to use it to dry socks and washcloths. I was afraid to use the dryer because I thought Ron would find out if it ran up the electric bill. That was dumb but I obeyed.

Ron also forbade me to use the phone. He told me he had a way of finding out if I did, so I never used it. If someone besides his mom called me, I was afraid to talk too long for fear he would find out. Sometimes Ron would call home and if the phone was busy, when he got home, he wanted to know who I had been talking to. When I told him his mom called, he would call her and ask if she actually did call. (I had to be very careful, because I took enough beatings without doing something on purpose.)

As much as Ron's mom cried and said she missed us, she would never come to our house to visit. At Easter she stopped by to deliver the Easter baskets for the little ones, but she never stayed very long at all. She always had someplace else to go and anyway we always went to visit my family on Easter. Easter was one of the few times that I got to spend with my family and my children got to spend time with their cousins.

When Barbara was about fourteen months old, we moved down the street to a different house. Our septic system was always backing up into the basement and it was getting harder and harder to do the laundry, so we had to move. The house we moved into had more room for all of us, and the neighbors told us that everyone who lived in the other house, always moved into this one after a while.

One thing I was never allowed to do was get the groceries. I always had to make a list for Ron, and once in a while he would let me go with him, especially if we needed something for the babies. There were times Ron would tell me that I had to meet him at the store. I had four babies and couldn't drive so I would put two of them in the stroller and two would walk beside me. It was at least a mile and a half to the store and these poor kids, Kenny was only two years old and Ronnie was four, just keep on walking. They were very good on our walks. When it was raining, we would catch a bus when we got to Dixie Highway. The bus stop was in front of the Greyhound Tavern restaurant. The grocery store was about another mile from there, and the kids were always worn out by then. We would ride back home with Ron.

Ron had always been telling me that President Kennedy would someday be shot. I had always humored him and said okay, and never thought much of it. One day, when we were still living in Crescent Springs, I was working in the kitchen and I heard on the television set that John F. Kennedy had been shot. I knelt on the floor in front of the television waiting to hear what was going on. I grabbed the phone up quickly and called Ron at work and told him what I had heard. He said he never heard that yet and hung up so that he could find out what was going on. I just sat there and listened to everything they were saying on the television.

Thank God the little ones were sleeping and I could pay attention. After about an hour, Ron finally called me back and said that all communication was shut down temporarily. He told me that they were all watching it at work and they were all very upset about what was happening.

It was awful and so sad that our President had been shot. Finally it was announced that he had died from the shots to the head. I knelt there and cried, because to me he was a great man. When Ron got home, that was all we talked about. We stayed glued to the television as much as possible for quite a few days, never wanting to miss any of what was going on. Even on the day that Oswald was shot, we were watching all that too. It was all so surreal. The day of the funeral, everything was so beautiful. Mrs. Kennedy was a wonderful example of dignity, poise, and grace. What an experience in history we were seeing and sad as it was, it was very moving. To this day, it is still stuck in my memory, where I was and what I was doing, when I heard that President Kennedy was shot.

We lived there in Crescent Springs until Ronnie turned six in March, and then we started discussing where we wanted to live and what school we wanted to send him to. I should say Ron decided, but we did discuss the plan this time.

We chose to look for a place in Alexandria because it was closer to his mom, and because he thought the parish school in Alexandria would be a good school for the kids. So we found a house for rent and moved to Alexandria. It was a nice little house, but kind of tiny. Ron kept saying we would not have to live there long, as he was going to buy a house. I never knew how we could even afford to buy one; he always said we had no money. I was never allowed to know what our money situation was. He was still buying the groceries, and he also took care of all the bills.

The first week we sent Ronnie to school, he was happy. I soon found out that he had the same nun who used to beat my brother in first grade at the orphanage. I was concerned for my son. Later, when I went to the first Mother's Club meeting and talked to her, I found out she liked Ronnie very much, and she said he was a very good student. I felt better. I didn't realize that the nuns would treat kids different who weren't in an orphanage.

One day, Ronnie didn't come home from school on time. I was worried and I called the school, and they said he left school walking like he always did. After about a half hour had gone by, I took the three little ones and I walked up the hill toward the school. At the top of the hill, there was some construction going on, and Ronnie had stopped to watch the men and the big diggers and forgot all about coming home. I really lit into him when we got him home. I was so worried that someone had taken him. They had us afraid of everything in the orphanage, and I still had all those fears. When his dad got home, Ronnie was really in trouble. It seemed like the more kids we had, the meaner Ron got to everyone.

After a while, I wasn't happy with the house, mainly because Ron made Ronnie and Kenny sleep in the upstairs room. The room was actually part of the attic that had been made into a bedroom. It was pretty far from where we slept, and these were little ones, and I just didn't like it. I thought they should be closer to me, but there was not enough room downstairs.

We had been living there for about three months when Thanksgiving came around. We always celebrated Thanksgiving Day with my family. On the following Sunday, we would go to visit Grandma Dotty and Grandpa Kiger, as the kids called them by now. This year, that Sunday just happened to fall on my birthday, November 29th. At six o'clock in the morning, the telephone woke us up. When I answered the phone, some man said, "Your house is on fire." I told him he was crazy and hung up. I started to climb back into bed and then I looked out the window. Sure enough there were fire trucks in front of the house. I told Ron, and he said I was crazy and just laid there.

I ran upstairs to see about the boys. Sure enough, the attic was on fire. I didn't think to get the kids out of the house first; I just tried to put out the fire. The whole time I was screaming for Ron to come help. Just that quickly, the firemen were in the house and yelling at me to get the kids out. At first, I didn't know where the boys were. I called for them, and when I found them hiding in the closet, I got them out right away and then got the girls out of the house. The only thing Ron was interested in was getting a white dress out of the house, that I had been making for his mom for a New Year's Eve dance. I t was to be a Christmas gift and he didn't want it to get smoke-filled.

The fire did some smoke and water damage to the upstairs of the home and I felt really bad about that. The boys had found one of their dad's cigarette lighters and piled up a bunch of insulation and used the lighter to set the fire. I was shocked that they would do such a thing. I knew that they hated sleeping upstairs but I had no idea that a child would pick up a lighter and start a fire. They got a severe tongue-lashing along with a good whipping from their dad. I felt so bad for the boys. What a mess we had. I had laundry hanging in the basement that got all wet from the firemen's hoses that had to be washed all over again. I had so much work to do and we still had to go to grandma's house for Thanksgiving dinner. Ron continued the boy's punishment at their grandma's house. I didn't think that was fair because I felt it was their dad's fault for leaving his lighter out. Ron's mom quickly put a stop to the punishment.

Another fire was hard to take. Thank God, the kids were okay, and we never lost any of our belongings this time.

The next day, the owners asked us to move out. I felt like they were saying we caused the fire on purpose and they asked us to move out right away. The owner was already unhappy with Ronnie because he had broken a window at their house a few months before. I felt then that she wanted us to move. She wasn't a happy lady anyway.

Ron started to look for another place to live right away. One evening, he came home and told me that he had found us a house to buy. I didn't know where he was going to get the money to buy it, or why he chose a place without even saying anything to me at all. I never got to see the house before he bought it. I was never allowed to make decisions involving money. I later found out that the house cost $14,900, and that was a lot back in 1963.

The house was about a mile and a half away from where we were living at the time. It had three bedrooms and a full basement, with a garage in the back of the home. It had a small front yard, and a small backyard that was flat for about seventy feet and then it went downhill. It was a pretty nice house. There were hardwood floors in the living room and bedrooms and a beautiful blue-and-white bathroom. The kitchen was very small, but that was all right. I had no choice in the decision, but I really liked the house. The kids would have to walk about two blocks to catch the school bus, but they were able to stay at the same school.

We were able to move in just two weeks before Christmas. It was fun trying to set up our own home for a change. We had three really nice bedrooms, one for our two baby girls and one for our two boys. The boys' room was a little small, but it worked out. I wanted the girls closer to me because they were still babies; one was three years old and the other was fifteen months old.

There wasn't much I had to do to the kitchen except put up curtains. The living room wasn't as easy. We had to pick out a paint color, which was hard; it was something we had never done before because you didn't get to paint rentals. Ron picked out a tan color, and I did the painting while he watched. It seemed like it took forever. We did not have paint rollers back then, all the painting was done with a brush, but I managed to get it done. It was great; we got the whole house set up, just in time for Christmas. We even put up a few decorations and lights outside.

On Christmas Eve, we would go to Grandma Dottie's to celebrate and the kids always got lots of presents. When we got back home I would get the tree set up for Christmas morning while the kids were sleeping. As usual, I was up all night getting it all set up and putting whatever toys together that had to be assembled. Ron would help for a while, but he always fell asleep. Still, I always managed to get it all done and get some sleep. I was so happy to see the kids' faces on Christmas morning. After breakfast we went to church and Ron went with us. He would go to church every once in a while now that Ronnie was in school.

In the afternoon, on Christmas day, it was time to go visit with my family. By now, Ron had stopped getting gifts for everyone but my youngest sister, who was our godchild. She was still small and always needed something. Even though he always said we were broke, and we couldn't spend any more money on the kids, he always managed to spend lots of money on gifts for me. He always bought me some really nice clothes, which was great, but I never had money of my own to buy a gift for him. I was shocked that he would buy so much for me, because he had said we were broke. I wanted him to spend any money we had on the kids. I always wanted more for the kids because we never got much for Christmas as kids and Christmas was for kids.

After we settled in on Oak Lane, there were times when I thought Ron was going somewhere and I would ask to go along. He always said "No, you can't possibly get the kids ready in time, and I need to be there now." After that, I learned to keep the diaper bag packed and the little ones ready to go. It worked most of the time, and I got out of the house for a short while.

There was a family who had moved in next door to us on the left that had six children. Some of the younger children were close to the same ages as my children, and they went to the same school. On the right side of our home was a family with one little boy about the same age as Ronnie. His mother hardly ever let him out unless she was there to watch him and I was the same way with my kids.

Ron had met lots of nice new friends, and they would all stand around and talk a lot after church. He soon got involved with his friends in getting a Knothole Baseball team together for the young boys in the Campbell County area, Ron enjoyed sports and this was good for him. A lot of the neighborhood kids played on his team, along with some of the young boys from the school.

In the fall, Ron also got very involved with peewee football in the area. A lot of the boys who played on his baseball team also played on his football team. Ronnie was on his Dad's teams and Kenny was able to play when he turned six. We were always running around all the time to all the different fields because of the different divisions the boys played in. It was great for me because I got to get out of the house but it was hard on Ronnie and Kenny. When they played ball, their dad, who was also their coach at this time, was very hard on them because he expected them to be the best.

After we were on Oak Lane for about a year, another family started building a house up the street from us. It was nice when they finally moved in. They had five children, three girls and two boys. Two of the girls were the same age as my girls, and the oldest boy was the same age of my oldest son Ronnie, and there were two younger ones.

The mother was a very sweet lady, named Pat, and we soon became good friends. Shortly after they moved in, she came and got me and told me that there was a snake in her baby's bedroom. She was deathly afraid of snakes and so was I. I hated snakes—but I never told her that. All the boys thought that it was funny; they were boys, and they were not afraid of snakes or anything. It was a small garden snake and I just got a stick and let it get on the stick and took it outside for her. She was so happy; she kept thanking me for getting rid of it.

Her children went to the same school as my children and I was happy that they were going to have some more friends at school their own age. A couple months after they moved in, Pat talked me into going to the PTA meetings with her. At first Ron wouldn't let me go with her but after a couple of months, he allowed me to ride up to the meetings with her. He said it was okay because he would not have to drive me. He did have to look after the kids. It wasn't his favorite thing to do, but they were getting older. Barbara, the baby at that time, was already three years old. By the time I left home it was almost their bedtime, so he didn't have to do much. That was a good thing.

With a lot of encouragement from Pat, I started getting involved in different things at school and started meeting other mothers. It was fun to get out of the house and I enjoyed being with all the other ladies because they were really sweet. Sometimes Pat would ask me to go to the store with her, and I told her I couldn't. I was not allowed, and she would say, "What do you mean you are not allowed?" Sometimes I would go if she promised to be back at a certain time, and she agreed. After a few trips like this, Ron found out one day. I told her that I couldn't go anymore because Ron would beat me if I did something he didn't allow me to do, and she said, "I will fix that." After that, if I went to the store with her, she made a habit of coming to our house on those evenings, just before Ron got home from work. She would be sitting there at the kitchen table and she would act like we had just been visiting with each other. Pat was a very friendly and funny lady, and she already knew Ron from Knothole Baseball because her son played on his team. When Ron walked in I was scared of what might happen. She would sit there and start teasing him about something and telling jokes, and they got along just great. Pat would stay there until she thought he would not be angry anymore, and most of the time it worked.

Ron had to deal with a lot parents who were always calling and asking to talk to him. After a while I would have to say which "Ron", because our son Ronnie's coaches were also calling for him. So it was then that I started calling Ron Mr. Stover or sometimes- just Stover. Some of the dads thought it was funny, so they started calling me Mrs. Stover.

One day, I said that I wanted to learn to drive a car, so three of my good friends decided it was time for me to learn. Pat Hartig, Lyda Caudill, and Pat Wiedeman all took turns teaching me how to drive. I could drive their cars because they weren't stick shifts like Ron's car. One time Pat W. took me out to practice parallel parking, she only had to take me out a couple of times and I got it. So she was the one who took me to try and get my license. I failed the first time, and I cried because they had put in so much time helping me. Pat W. didn't get discouraged like I did; she just took me back and the second time and I passed. I was so happy, I couldn't thank them all enough for all their help, and they were very happy for me. Now I could drive, but I still couldn't drive a "stick-shift car so I had no car to drive.

One day out of the blue, Mr. Stover came home with a beautiful aqua blue and white car that was automatic, not a stick shift. That was great because I could drive it. One of the first things I did with that beautiful car was get too close to a telephone pole and scraped the whole side of the car. I felt terrible and I was afraid to go home and let Ron see it. I knew there was "hell" to pay and I deserved it.

It was not long after I had a car that I could drive, that our television went out. We couldn't afford a new one and Stover's aunt said she had one that she would give us, if he would come pick it up. Stover made me go get the TV from his aunt who lived in Independence. It was a dark snowy night and the roads were very icy. I was scared to death to drive in the snow, let alone in icy conditions, so I had to take one of the boys with me. He had to have a TV so he could lie on the couch and watch whatever he wanted to watch.

Sometimes I had to take the kids to the doctor so Stover would let me take the car. First I had to take him to work, which was in Ohio. I got up early in the morning with the little kids and drove him to work, and I had to be back on time to pick him up after work. I was there early every time because I was not going to get in trouble for being late. Sometimes I would use the car to take Stover's mom shopping. After I had taken Stover to work in Cincinnati, I had to go all the way to Ross to pick her up. We then went back to Cincinnati to shop and then drove all the way back to Ross and dropped her off. Then I had to be back in time to pick Stover up at work. That was a lot of running especially with three little ones. It was expected of me but I really did not mind because I liked my mother-in-law. One time I had a low tire, and I stopped at the gas station to get it fixed. They took the tire off and fixed it and we went on our way. Just as we rounded the next turn in the road, the tire fell off the car. Here I was sitting on the side of the road with Stover's mom and three little ones in a broken-down car. We started walking back to the service station carrying the kids. A policeman came along and took us back to the service station, and they went and got the car and fixed it right. They had forgotten to tighten the lug nuts. That was my second mishap with a car and it was very scary.

Chapter 8

Out of the blue, I was pregnant again after three-and-a-half years. My neighbor Lyda was also pregnant. It was neat having someone to talk to about the new baby and what we were both going through together. Pat was a wonderful friend, and she was excited for both of us. In the past, I was always embarrassed when I was pregnant but this time, it felt different. I had a lot of good friends who cared for me, and I realized that it was okay to be pregnant, I was married. It was also such a blessing to be having another baby. I always said I wanted six. Our baby was due in December.

That summer, Stover had gotten me an old car to drive. When football started up again, I was in charge of getting the boys to Fort Thomas to practice when Mr. Stover didn't want to come home from work. He would go straight to the field so he could get started on time. No wonder he had gotten me a little old car. Oh well. It was a funny-looking boxy thing that was black and white, but I didn't care—it was a good running car. It would get us all around, and I also enjoyed picking up the children whose parents were still at work. Since I was pregnant, I was getting bigger, so I was lucky to fit behind the wheel of the car. The parents always showed up and took their kids home after practice.

Those were hectic times, running around all the time from field to field. The boys, because of their ages, played at different times and places. Mr. Stover was in charge of scheduling the games, but he couldn't always get the games scheduled in the same area. It kept me busy, running everywhere. I liked being busy; it was what I was used to.

Our youngest son, Christopher, was born on December 9th, 1966 all nine pounds, five ounces of precious baby boy. He wasn't quite as chubby as the two older boys, even though he weighed more. He was perfect. Our neighbor had her little boy around the same time. What a Christmas gift. Stover and I still had to go shopping for Christmas for the kids, so we had to take Chris with us when he was only a week old. It was cold out, but I didn't want to leave him home with the other children who were only four, five, six, and eight. I got the neighbor girl to baby-sit them for me. When Chris was born, we wanted to name him Chris after Stover's "Aunt" Chris, who we all loved. So we named him Christopher Michael Charles. Stover's mom insisted we throw the name Charles in there after Ron's great-uncle Charlie, who seldom came around. It all went together, so I agreed.

The first time we went to Grandma's after Chris was born, I had everything in the car—even the diaper bag—and forgot to take the baby with me. We hadn't even gotten out of the driveway when I remembered and I never did live that down. Grandpa Kiger was always teasing me about leaving Chris.

We had Chris baptized at our parish church right after Christmas along with my niece, Cindy who was five years old at the time. I was glad she was getting baptized. When Cindy was a baby, Joan and I thought that she was too tiny and frail; we were afraid she might not make it. So one day at my sister's home, we kind of baptized her ourselves. She turned out to be healthy after all; we were always worried my sister Shirley would not have her baptized, so we were happy when it finally came about.

Once when Chris was about six weeks old, I did a really dumb thing. The kids were driving me nuts and I had to get supper fixed and have it ready for Stover when he walked in the door. They were all crying and fighting, so I made all four of them sit in separate corners and be quiet. Barbara hated it when I did this to them, because she knew she would always fall asleep, and she did not want to go to sleep. I told them if they didn't behave, I would put Chris in the oven. I must have been really crazy that day. I said I was sorry for saying such a stupid thing; I felt bad for a really long time. I would have never hurt any one of my kids intentionally. I loved them dearly—they were all that was important to me. I must have had the baby blues, as they called it back then. I never told Stover, though I already felt bad that I wasn't able to protect my kids from their dad. The children never told either, because I had learned not to say things to them like "Don't tell your father what had happened today." If I didn't bring it up to them, they never said a word. It was when I would say, "Don't tell" that they would tattle every time. That was a lesson I learned the hard way from my children.

Shortly after Chris was born, Stover's demeanor seemed to change a little around the house. He was still mean to the children and me, but not quite as often. He always treated Kenny worst of all, and he still continued to say that Kenny wasn't his kid. He would pick Kenny up by the shirt and yell at him and throw him on the couch and make him sit for what seemed like hours.

I would spank the children on their bottoms and get after them, after a while, I thought to myself, *these are just little children. They should not be treated like we were treated in the orphanage. We were just kids too, and that wasn't a good thing.*

Stover didn't smack me around anymore in front of the kids. He would do it in our bedroom after the kids went to sleep. Most of the time I never knew what I did to upset him, and he always had to tell me. It was usually something very stupid; maybe I never ironed his handkerchiefs right or didn't have his socks folded right, or maybe I talked to someone on the phone he didn't want me talking to. Then he would go back in the living room and lie on the couch and sleep until eleven o'clock.

I would tell him to go to bed, and he would say he wasn't ready yet, even though he was sleeping. If I tried to watch anything on the television that wasn't what he wanted to watch, he would yell at me and tell me to turn it back to his station, even though he was sleeping and not really watching it. We were lucky just to have one television.

I would go to bed and fall asleep, and sometimes Stover would come in and wake me up just to mess around. He didn't seem interested in me any other time. He wouldn't cuddle with me on the couch, and he never wanted to kiss me, but that was okay with me. He was always shoving me away. Sometimes he would tell me he was going to kill me and he would start choking me. Many times I went to bed not knowing whether or not I was going to be alive in the morning. All I could do was lay there quietly and pray and pretend I didn't care anymore. The next day he would always apologize and say it would never happen again. But it did, it happened over and over again. He just never would let me get a full night's sleep either. Between Ron and the kids, I never got too much sleep; if the children even whimpered the least little bit, he would shove me out of bed and tell me to shut them up.

When Chris was one year old I got back into the swing of things at the Mother's Club meetings. We would have bazaars at Christmastime, and we would fashion homemade treasures from scratch; like the ornaments that we made out of eggshells, Tide, and water. You would make a paste with the Tide and spread it around an eggshell with an opening in front, then put cotton inside and glue a lovely Christmas scene inside the opening and put cotton and glitter on the outside. They were beautiful. We also sewed many things to sell, like Barbie-doll clothes, aprons, and Christmas-tree skirts, anything we could think of to sell to make money for the school. We would also have a bazaar in the spring and sometimes in the fall. One year we had a fashion show, with a luncheon and prizes, mostly donated by businesses in the area. I modeled two outfits in the show. This was when Chris was almost two years old and I was still small enough to wear these nice outfits.

When Chris was around two years old, I started telling Stover that I wanted a divorce. This time he said go ahead. "You are an unfit mother anyway, and I will just have the kids taken away from you." I did not want him to take my children from me, and naturally I thought he could, so I had to back off. I would go through anything to keep my kids. No one was going to take my children from me like our parents allowed us to be taken. Not even their own dad.

Stover was good at convincing me that I was a terrible person, but I never knew why I was terrible. I did everything I was told. At this point, I couldn't talk to anyone about getting a divorce. I knew it was against our religion, and I didn't know how my friends would feel about it. I was also afraid that one of them would tell Stover that I talked about it and he would beat me again, so I kept quiet.

Stover always made everything sound like the law was on his side. He would remind me that his aunt worked for a lawyer, so I thought he was right. I just didn't know any better, and I was too afraid to go up against him. I may not have been the best mother in the world, but the kids were mine; I loved them very much, and I did my best.

I let it go then and after a while, he started saying *he* was going to divorce *me* as soon as he got all of the bills paid. I didn't know what bills we had, so I never knew how long that might take. Besides I never really wanted a divorce, I just wanted him to get counseling.

As Chris got a little older, he was allowed to do things the other kids weren't allowed to. Chris could drink his dad's soft drinks and Stover never said a word. If one of the other kids did it, they would get in big trouble. The older kids got to the point where they would ask Chris to get a soft drink just so they could have a drink. They never got caught, and I never told on them either, because I knew they would be in trouble for something stupid. Chris never got into trouble with his dad, and I was glad. But I always thought it was very strange, and I was glad, that he wasn't mean to him like he was to the older kids.

I was always making clothes for my girls and every time I would sew, Pat Hartig would ask me to make some for her girls too. She would get the material, and I would make what I could. I even made shorts with the little skirt in the front called skorts. It eventually got to the point where Pat wanted me to sew clothes for her. She was a little heavy, and I had one pattern for her that always worked. When she wanted something fancy, we used the same pattern and bought fancy material and dressed it up. No one knew it was always the same pattern except for Pat and me. There were two other ladies in the neighborhood who had also asked me to make dresses for them. It felt good that I could actually do something that well to please someone else, and they were very happy that the dresses always fit them very well. When my younger sister Gerry got married, I made her wedding dress. She wanted something sweet and simple and she looked great. (I also got to make a wedding dress for her daughter Maria years later.)

One time Pat Hartig, Lyda, and I decided to go on a diet after our baby boys were born. It was comical, because we would get together once a week for a weigh-in and then sit around and have coffee and donuts. We always had a really good time. Pat stayed on her diet for quite a while and lost a lot of weight. On her birthday, I decided to make a fake round cake out of cardboard and then I iced and decorated it. I made it look real fancy and even wrote "Happy Birthday Pat" on it. Pat was so excited that I had made her a cake, and she loved it. When she tried to cut into it, we all burst out laughing and so did she, and then afterwards she teasingly called us a few choice names. We told her we did not want to mess up her diet, but we did have a real cake on the side that the kids were patiently waiting to dig into. Pat was a wonderful friend and I dearly loved her.

Two other friends of mine helped out around the rectory, and one day they asked me if I would like to help them. Sometimes the priest wanted help with little things that needed painting and various little things that he said needed a woman's touch. I enjoyed working with these particular ladies and they were very good to me. We actually painted a whole room for this one priest, and he was pleased with the job we had done for him.

The older kids were in school when I helped out at the rectory but I always had Chris with me. He was a tiny little one, for a two year old, and he was always so good. You could sit him down and give him something to write on or play with, and he was never any trouble for us. Sometimes I would call him my little angel.

It was around this time that our mom met the most wonderful guy, named Bill Beahr. He was very nice to all of our mom's kids and grandchildren, and we all liked him immediately. Bill wanted to marry our mom, but she would not get an annulment so that they could marry in the church. She wouldn't budge, so he eventually gave up on insisting that she get an annulment.

My older sister Joan tried talking Bill out of marrying our mom. She said our mom was not reliable and liked men too much. He said he didn't care, because he loved her. Five months later, they were married in the priest's parlor. Bill warned all of us to be on time. I tried really hard to get five kids ready on time and Stover was no help. I even had to help Stover get himself ready. We wound up being ten minutes late, and we missed most of the ceremony. I never heard the end of it from my new stepfather, and he constantly teased me about being late.

This was our mom's third marriage, and Bill eventually became known as "Grandpa Beahr" to the grandkids. He was such a nice guy, and we all enjoyed him. We all felt like he was the father we never had. Bill always treated us like we were one of his own kids. He took the time to talk to us, which was something our mom never did. She did not seem to be comfortable around any of us, except for Sandy, who was never sent to the orphanage. I'm guessing she had no guilt where Sandy was concerned.

Our Mom and Step-Dad

Bill sold his home in Ohio and moved into my grandpa's house with our mom and several of her younger children. Our mom had been living with her dad, our grandpa, for several years. Before our mom moved into grandpa's house, it was always kept neat and clean. After she moved in, with so many living there, it was always a mess. When Bill moved in, he got the home in very neat order, and the kids kept it that way. My grandpa was very happy about that. He could see that Bill was a good reliable man.

Everyone but Sandy listened to Bill. Sandy had a mind of her own, and our mom would not allow Bill to correct her. Even the older kids could not get her to behave. She would come home from school for lunch and never go back to school. Bill and the older kids tried to get her to go back to school, but our mom would only scold Bill.

Bill began inviting us married children to our grandpa's house. The house was once again neat and clean and felt like a home. We always had such good visits with Bill, and I loved seeing my grandpa. Our mom didn't talk to us much, but we didn't care. Bill always included us in all the conversations and cared about what we had to say. He was so good to us.

Bill would even wait on us when we visited. He made us feel more wanted than we ever had. It seemed someone finally cared. My sisters and brothers and I would often discuss how wonderful he was. We all felt exactly the same way. Bill would make sure the house was clean and made sure the younger kids still living at home all had food.

I'm sure it was hard on him taking on someone else's children, teenagers at that. After all, his own two children were all grown up. Some of the kids who lived with our mom worked, and that was a big help too. Bill didn't have to do it all, but he probably would have. He was that good of a man. He loved our mom, but sometimes he would say to some of us, "After what your mom did to you children, I don't understand why you all are still good to her." We didn't know any better, we were always taught to be respectful to others.

111

My Grandpa with four of my five children, 1967

Our grandpa died at the age of eighty-six, and he left the house to our mom and Bill. I didn't think it was fair to her brothers and sisters, but I guess he did it because she was the only one who did not have a home of her own. Our mom was still working at this time, and when we stopped by to see her at work, we could tell she loved her job. She enjoyed flirting with all the men in particular and having fun with everyone she worked with.

My children had two really wonderful grandpas in their life, and both grandpas loved them like they were their own flesh and blood. My children never knew they were actually their step-grandparents until after they reached their teens. It just never came up, and we never thought to discuss it. When they found out, they were pleasantly surprised, because both grandpas were very good to all the children and the children really loved them. I always felt really good about that.

When Chris was about three, we thought he might have a hearing problem, so I took him to a hearing specialist. During the testing, they couldn't get him to understand what they wanted him to do, because he was only three years old. They told me to bring him back when he could understand what they needed him to do. So we waited.

Sometimes Stover and I would go to dances at the school, like New Year's and other dances. The girls hated it when we left them with the boys. Ronnie and Ken gave them a hard way to go all the time. One summer we went to an outdoor dance. I loved to dance and Ron didn't, so he just sat at the table and smoked and listened to a ballgame on the radio. I was always out dancing with others and visiting the other tables and having lots of fun for a change. Stover was being a stick-in-the-mud, but at least he let me go.

At one of the outdoor dances, I was out on the floor dancing to "Proud Mary". This was a great song to dance to, and I was having a lot of fun. When I got back to the table, Ron was gone and no one knew where he was. I eventually figured out he went home without me. He just left me there. My sister and her husband were with us, and I told them I could walk home, it wasn't that far—about two miles. They insisted on taking me home. All of our friends' were kind of surprised because they had never seen Stover do anything like that before.

Stover was still involved in Knothole Baseball and peewee football.

It was around this time that one of the mothers from the team wanted to have a banquet for Stover, for all the good he was doing with the kids. She had a banquet in his honor at the bar she owned in Newport. She had food catered along with snacks and drinks. A lot of the kids showed up, but there were very few parents there. I was actually feeling bad that more parents did not show up.

It was right after the party that he decided to quit being involved in the sports programs, he was done helping with sports altogether. That was also the end of sports for our boys. They weren't really interested in playing ball any way. After that, the only time Stover played ball was in the backyard with Ronnie and Kenny, or out at grandma Dot's. The boys finally lost interest in sports altogether.

My Family in 1970

Chapter 9

Chris was almost four years old, when out of the blue, Stover said he was sick and dying. Now, mind you, this was a man who never went to a doctor, or hardly ever let me take our kids to one. Stover told me that he had myelogenous leukemia, and without experimental treatments he would probably die. I was not allowed to tell anyone, especially his mom. I knew what Leukemia was, because that is what his grandma had died from, so I knew it was bad. As far as I knew, he never had any signs of being sick, or ever mentioned feeling bad, so this was a total shock to me.

Back then, the milkman delivered your milk, and the insurance man came to your door to collect on your insurance payments for the month. Both the milkman and insurance man were our friends from church and baseball. After a while, I started talking to them about what was going on. I was always so upset, and they were always good listeners. They didn't understand how Stover could be sick because he surely didn't look sick. A few weeks later I told my neighbors. I didn't care how much he told me to keep my mouth shut. I needed to discuss this with someone. It was a puzzle, and it got worse as time went on. Stover was being very secretive and would not let me speak to his doctor.

That summer, we were getting a new pastor at our church that my friend Pat knew very well. She suggested I talk to the pastor about Stover, and that he would get Stover to go back to church. That was all fine, but that it wasn't what I was concerned about at the time. I just wanted Stover to let me go to an appointment with him so I could hear from the doctor exactly what was going on. This went on for months and months. One time he told me he had to go to Chicago for an experiment and he only had a 10 percent chance of living and he wouldn't let anyone go with him. When I was alone, I cried a lot. I never really knew what was going on. Eventually Stover told his mom what was going on, and his mom and stepdad talked him into letting them go with him to Chicago. He never let them go to the hospital with him, and they ended up staying at the hotel. Soon after that trip, his stepdad started to question, if this was real, or what was really going on with Stover. When he came home from Chicago, he had some kind of contraption taped to his inner arm. He said it was so the doctor could put medication into it and not have to stick him all the time with needles. It didn't even look like it went into his arm. I never knew they would let you leave the hospital with something like that in your arm. It was all beginning to look real stupid. My friends and I would talk about it all the time, and they could not understand it either. Stover also told me he had to go the hospital and get blood. At first I thought nothing of it, but the more my friend Pat and I talked, the more we thought it was weird.

I started going to Mass during the week. At least I could walk there when I had no car. I would ask Jesus to help me to understand why it was such a problem that he could not tell me what was going on. Why tell me anything in the first place if I was to know nothing else? It was driving me crazy. One night when he told me he had to go to the hospital to get blood, I called Pat and told her what was going on. At that time, I didn't have a car to drive, and she said, "Come on, Marian, we are going to follow him." And that is just what we did. I couldn't have gotten through this ordeal without my friend Pat. She was always there for me.

After we got to the hospital, we saw him walking in the emergency doors. We went inside the hospital and asked the employees if they had seen him because he told us he had needed to get blood. They told us that no one had come in. We told them that we saw him go through the door as we were pulling in, and they again said that no one came in that they saw. So we figured he must have gone in one door and out through another one. It was really strange. He was home when we got back, and we never said anything to him. This seemed like it went on forever and he continued doing really odd things.

Finally the new pastor, Father Ott, arrived at our parish. I was already working around the rectory with some of my friends and I would run into him once in a while. One day he stopped to talk to us, and he suggested I come up and talk to him sometime about Stover, so I did. Our talk just got me another job up at church and Father Ott as a new friend.

I started counting money on Mondays with three ladies that I became really good friends with. It was so much fun and it took my mind off Stover for a while. I was allowed to bring Chris with me, who was tiny for a four-old. Father had given him the nickname of "Peanut" because he was so small. Chris was so well-behaved, you hardly knew he was around.

Father Ott finally got around to talking to Mr. Stover but it didn't do any good. I still didn't get to go to the doctor with him. Stover even went to the extreme of tearing the pages out of the encyclopedia on leukemia so that I couldn't find out anything about it. I cried and worried all the time. I just could not figure out what he was up to. Why was Stover doing this to our family? What was he trying to do to us? It was all so unreal. All I really needed to do was talk to the doctor and get to the bottom of this problem. Stover was always such a good liar, and I could not trust him. I needed answers. I needed to figure this out.

I had been working in the Library at school two days a week and I became good friends with the nun who was in charge of the library. I really enjoyed working around the children and I could take Chris with me. The teachers and the nuns always enjoyed seeing Chris. At school the teachers and nuns had all the school children praying for Stover and our family.

The next thing I knew, I wound up with another job up at church—cleaning the church with two of my dear friends, Dorothy and Rosemary. (To this day, I still have a bracelet Dorothy gave me that she had engraved, "To my best friend.")

I loved cleaning the church. It reminded me of the little chapel I cleaned so many times at the orphanage. I loved being close to the Lord; he was always there for me to talk to. Of course, he was always everywhere anyway, but he just seemed much closer when I was in church, and it was so peaceful there.

This business of not talking to a doctor about Stover's "illness" went on for what I thought was forever. It was driving me crazy, and of course I was driving my friends and Father Ott crazy too, questioning them all the time. I knew I was stubborn, but Stover was even worse. There seemed to be no reason for keeping me in the dark like that—it was crazy. I was so sick and tired of not getting any answers from my own husband. After he had been "sick" for so long, one of my friends came to me and asked what treatment Stover was getting and what doctors he was seeing. She wanted to know what was keeping him alive for so long a time. Her husband had been diagnosed with the same illness, and he was going downhill very fast and Stover was still able to work and didn't seem sick.

I finally went to our family doctor, who was the main doctor on staff at St. Luke Hospital in Fort Thomas. I discussed Stover's illness with him, and he told me point blank, "Right now we have no patients being treated at this hospital with leukemia." He said he would know if there was someone with the disease, and he would tell me. That really sent me off thinking. I went to my friend Pat and told her. We both figured he was just trying to drive me nuts—it's called "mental cruelty." I just couldn't figure out what he was doing or why. I couldn't divorce him. He always threatened to take my kids away from me and tell everyone I was an unfit mother, even though he always told his mom and everyone else that I was an excellent mother. He could make everyone believe him, and I believed he could do it. His family could do anything they wanted because his aunt worked for a criminal lawyer and he let me know it. "The law is always on my side," he would say.

Chapter 10

Finally, after all the ups and downs, I had had it. I guess it just had to happen. One day I woke up in a very dark room. It was very quiet, and I had no idea where I was. I was told that I was in the hospital, and I'd had a nervous breakdown. I had tried to kill myself. I guess I did not do a very good job. The worst part was that they told me that Chris was home alone with me, and he was only four years old. The other kids were in school. To this day, I have no idea what set me off like that. Chris told me afterward that I had locked all the doors and told him not to let anyone in. Apparently he did not listen, thank God. No one was allowed to visit me for a while, and when they were allowed in, it was only with my permission. Of course, Stover was there soon after I woke up. He was my "husband," so he was allowed.

There was a basket of fruit on my stand that someone had sent. I got lots of cards from my children and all my good friends. Some of the schoolchildren, teachers and nuns from our parish school also sent cards.

I was very heavily sedated, and they were giving me shock treatments. I understand my sister Gerry and her husband Bill came to the house to watch my children while I got better. I stayed in the hospital for a week or more; I lost track of time. I did not know what time of year it was, and I wanted to be with my children. I missed them so much. I know it was around Easter when I got home. I remember we were at his mom's, and my sister-in-law was fixing my daughters' hair for them. It was Easter Sunday, and I got upset and told her they were *my* girls. I wanted to do it myself.

Stover took us to his parents' house when I did come home from the hospital, and we stayed there for a short while. The kids had been fine with my little sister while I was gone. I got letters from them telling me how much they missed me and wanted me to come home. It took me a long time to recover from that situation. It felt like months before I could think for myself. They had me on all kinds of stupid drugs. I wasn't even used to taking an aspirin, and I never had a headache until then.

After I left the hospital, I had to continue to go to a psychiatrist, and he always wanted to do shock treatments on me like I had when I was in the hospital. They were horrible—they did nothing for me. The psychiatrist told me I had a very "stubborn mind." *Why?* I wondered. *Because I tried to survive in spite of everything I had been through as a child, and now even more so that my husband was treating me like I was an idiot?*

I guessed when the doctors talked to me, I had told them about Stover and how "sick" he was supposed to be and how upset I was over not knowing what was going on with him. Stover was telling them that it wasn't true and that he was fine, and he didn't know what I was talking about, he was not sick. They believed him, he said, because he was sane and I was the crazy one. That was just the kind of thing he would do to me.

About a month after I left the hospital, Stover came home from work and told me that they wanted to put me away downstate, lock me up, and throw away the key because I was that crazy. He even told me he started sending donations to the St. Jude Society, patron saint of hopeless cases. My good friends and my family knew I wasn't crazy, and they supported me. I was very grateful for all of them.

At my next appointment with the psychiatrist, he saw that I got upset and he told me he wanted to do a third shock treatment on me. He had asked a question about our parents. When he asked the question I thought about how our parents didn't want any of us, and how it hurt that our mom was never there for us. He didn't even try to discuss why I was upset, he just ordered another shock treatment for the following week

I thought about it all the way home, and by the time I got home I decided I was not going back to this quack anymore. I took myself off all the medication because I felt like I was not "me" anymore and I got on with my life on my own.

During this time, Stover did do some work around the house. He actually painted the living-room ceiling for me. He had never done any type of work like this around the house before. I always did the painting, all the yard-work, and any repairs that needed to be done around the house.

The summer after my breakdown, Stover decided to take us on a trip to give me a "break." He bought a used pop-up camper from our neighbor that needed a lot of work. I worked hard patching the canvas cover and I also did a lot of cleaning to make it presentable. Stover decided we needed to go to the Smoky Mountains and camp for a week. The campground had a swimming pool and a playground area, which was perfect for the kids. It was not a "break" for me; seven people in a small pop-up camper, the outdoor cooking, and cleaning up after everyone was no fun for me, it was a job. He would not even think of going to a restaurant on the trip.

On the way home, we stopped at Cumberland Falls. The falls were beautiful. The ride down and back, on the other hand, was terrible, with him doing all the driving. It was not a pleasant trip for me, but the kids enjoyed it so I was happy for them.

It was time for Chris to start kindergarten, and he was very upset because he did not get to go to the same school with his brothers and sisters. Our parish school had cancelled kindergarten and first-grade classes for lack of teachers and

Chris had been looking forward to going there. When I counted money for the church I would let him walk to the school cafeteria to get chocolate milk and the cafeteria ladies would also give him cookies.

During Chris's first three days of school at Campbell County, they had to call me because they could not get him to stop crying. They tried giving him ice cream and anything they could think of to get him to stop crying. I had to go get him, and I could not talk him into staying either. I wound up taking him home. I thought it was because he wanted to go to the kids' school. When I took him back on the fourth day, they gave him a different teacher, and he was fine from there on out. We figured he was afraid of the first teacher; she was an older teacher, and Chris apparently did not like her. After that, he was fine and he had no more problems at school.

We had learned when Chris was about three years old that he had a hearing problem. He couldn't say *t* or *s*, and he called ice cream "hopum." When he started school, they did put him in special classes because of his speech and hearing problems.

When he was finally able to go to the parish school, he was so happy. He wanted to be in the same school with his sisters and brothers. They immediately asked about his hearing problem and insisted that he go to a hearing specialist. The specialist figured he had a 60 percent hearing loss in one ear and a 40 percent loss in the other. Chris was fitted for hearing aids at the age of seven. They were very annoying for him, even though he could hear well. The children would hit him on the side of the head just to hear the hearing aids whistle, and it annoyed Chris. He had to sit by the window to block other sounds in the room so he could hear without all the background noises. He did pretty well in school otherwise. He was a good kid and very helpful to the teachers and others. He couldn't wait to make his First Communion, and he was always trying to trick the priest into giving him the Host at the Communion rail. Most of the priests knew him and knew better. One day, when Chris went up to Communion with me, there was a different priest, and he gave the Host to Chris. Chris came back to the pew smiling. He was a little shit.

Everything at home seemed to be fine for a while. Stover's "illness" wasn't mentioned again unless we were around his mom. His mom always believed everything he told her. I wasn't allowed to talk about his illness or tell her anything about his health. I still obeyed some of his orders.

By this time Chris was seven years old and the kids were all in school. I went out and got me a paying job that would keep me busy. I always enjoyed working and this way I would have a few dollars to spend. I went to work at a pizza parlor right up the street from the church. I had never heard of pizza until they brought a pizza parlor to Alexandria. I still cleaned the church with my good friend Florence. Rosemary and Dorothy had retired after I had my breakdown. Florence and I had a good time keeping that church neat and clean. I also continued to count the money on Mondays with my good friends, Mary, Nellie, and Elaine. Doing these jobs helped keep me sane.

Once when I was at work at the pizza place, I had my daughter Dorothy put a roast in the oven for their supper. Dorothy put it in the oven and she went out to play and forgot all about it. Stover was home on the couch watching TV sound asleep. The roast was burned to a crisp. I could not understand how Stover could not smell the smoke from the roast burning. The house still smelled of smoke and burnt roast when I got home from work at eleven. Dorothy got in big trouble for not being more responsible, but she was only a kid. I got very upset with Stover and jumped all over him. Why couldn't he be more responsible and check on the food himself? He was the grown-up, and I told him so. I was furious with him. He was never responsible around the house; he never tried. The only one that mattered to him was him self. I finally got to the point where I could talk back without getting slapped around—he was too lazy to get up off the couch.

While I was working at Pasquale's, they hired this young seventeen-year-old guy named Ted. He was a very good, and responsible worker. He was six feet tall and very light on his feet, it seemed like he walked around on his tiptoes. He loved to work on cars and make them look really sharp. After a while, Ted and I became good friends. After work we would get a pizza, he would get his beer, and we would sit in the car and talk before going home. He was like one of my kids.

I never drank before, except for a little wine once in a while but eventually I would have one of his beers. It was fun for me. Stover was furious that I had been drinking, but I didn't care anymore. It kind of became a routine—pizza and beer after work to relax.

After Ted was working there for a while, he finally got to meet my younger kids, Chris, Barbara, and Dorothy. A couple months later, Ted said to me, "Hey, someday I am going to marry your daughter." I laughed at him but I didn't think to ask which one. My girls were only fourteen and fifteen, so I told him that they couldn't date until they were sixteen anyway. I just thought he was being funny.

Kenny and Ronnie were sixteen and eighteen by this time and they decided they did not have to listen to me anymore. I couldn't get them to do anything around the house, not even take the garbage out. They would argue with me, and we would be screaming back and forth. Their dad was no help, so I gave up. One day when I was doing the laundry, I found a bag of "pot" in one of the boys' pants pockets. That evening I asked the boys if it belonged to them and neither one would claim it. So I sat down in the middle of the floor and rolled the pot in cigarette papers like I used to roll cigarettes for our dad. I acted like I was smoking it but I couldn't even stand the smell of cigarette smoke. I didn't really smoke it; I just wasted it by letting it burn it self out. Mr. Stover, Ted and the boys just sat there and laughed. They thought it was funny. In the morning, when the girls heard about it, they were shocked (appalled, they said) because they heard their mom was smoking pot. A few weeks later, one of the boys told me that I wasted $25 dollars worth of pot. Oh well, I thought.

One afternoon when I was getting ready for work, Ronnie told me he had to be at work around the same time I did. He did not let me know soon enough, or I could have driven him to work first. That evening when I got off work, my car was missing. I was shocked and mad. I called the police, and later when they called back they let me know that my son had taken my car so that he could go to work. So I got Ted to drive me home.

The man, who owned the building that I worked in, was a judge and we were on good terms. I told him about what my son had done, and he suggested that I not let him get away with it. So I pressed charges and went to court just to teach him a lesson. The judge gave him a good scolding. Soon after that incident, Ronnie started spending a lot of time at his grandma's house in Ross after school. It was close to his work and he didn't have to deal with his dad or me.

One night, after work, while Ted and I were sitting in the car, I told Ted that I always had a fear that my steering wheel would come off when I was driving. I always tried to lift it up whenever I got in the car to see if it would pull off. To show him what I meant, I pulled up on the steering wheel—and it pulled right off? For a second, Ted and I both looked at each other in shock, then we started laughing about it. Suddenly we both got to thinking that maybe someone had loosened it on purpose. Ted tightened the wheel nut and decided to follow me home that night to make sure I got there safely.

When I though about it later I really did wonder if Stover had something to do with it, and I got a little scared. Stover always used to take the plugs off the car if he thought I might be trying to go out by myself. I soon figured out what he did to the car so that it wouldn't start, so I got me an extra set of plugs. I was ready the next time he took the plugs off. I could put the plugs back in the car without going back in the house. The first time I replaced the plugs, he chased me down the street in his pajamas, like he was going to catch me. I just kept on driving. Eventually he got tired of taking the plugs out.

I didn't care by then how much trouble I would be in with him. I was getting smarter and learning how to deal with him. I had friends who told me I did not have to live that way anymore. The priest would never have said that, but my friends did. One of the priests wanted to know what *I did* to make Stover angry enough to hit me. Nothing! I tried doing everything so I would not get hit. All I did was try to be a good wife and mother. I didn't like being hit but I didn't know how to stop it. I was almost ready to move forward with the divorce. I was still afraid he would seriously hurt me, so I never let my guard down.

We were beginning to have problems at home with the furnace and some other things that needed fixing, and Stover was no handyman. He would only keep enough oil in the tank for it to run a day at a time. That was not good for the furnace. Sometimes there would often be a big *boom* in the night because there was mud on the bottom of the oil tank, and it would clog up and blow. He would take the motor apart and try to clean and fix the parts at the kitchen table. The whole house stunk of oil.

One evening when I was at choir practice, Kenny showed up with blood all over his face. He said that his dad made him get on his bike with a five-gallon can and ride on the main highway to the gas station to get oil. Kenny had a wreck because of the weight of the oil and split his chin open. I had to take him to the hospital, and he had to have fourteen stitches in his chin. I was so mad when I got home. I yelled at Stover and told him he should have asked me to pick up the oil. I was so upset and I didn't care if he did hit me for hollering at him.

After working at Pasquale's for several years, I decided I was going to need more money if I was ever going to be serious about getting a divorce and caring for my kids on my own. The kids were older, and I didn't think he could take them away from me anymore. I started thinking that maybe the kids might not want to live with him because they knew how he was by now.

By this time Ted had gotten himself a full-time job at the same place where Stover worked. I was also trying to find a full-time job so I talked to a lot of people who came into Pasquale's about places to work. I decided I would like to try getting a job in a nursing home. I loved working with people, and the nursing home wasn't far away. I also knew a couple of people who worked there. I applied, and after two weeks they called me. I needed to take a six-week course in nurse's-aide training during the day from seven o'clock in the morning to three in the afternoon. That worked out, because the kids got home at four o'clock. Once the course was over, I wanted to start working the night shift. I could still clean the church in the mornings and count money for the parish, which was one of my favorite things to do with my friends Mary, Nellie, and Elaine. I really enjoyed the time we spent together.

The training at the nursing home went really well. They told us in the beginning that all of us would not make it, that we might be too squeamish, or not cut out for this type of work. I did great; I loved working with the elderly people. At first it was hard—I didn't know you had to lie to some of the patients because they had Alzheimer's. I know it was to protect them, but I felt bad about it.

I couldn't wait to get on the night shift, because I was leery of feeding patients. I had a fear of them choking on me and I wouldn't be able to help them. I didn't like helping them take baths either. I was always afraid of hurting one of them.

I liked the night shift much better. I worked eleven at night until seven in the morning, when almost everyone was in bed—that worked out good. Coming home from work in the morning got to be fun. Chris always knew what time I would be home and he would hide behind the door to scare me, or so he thought. He was an early bird, always in bed and asleep by nine o'clock and up in the morning at six. He was so sweet and silly.

I made sure the kids got off to school before going to clean the church. Then I would go home and got a few hours of sleep.

Eventually I worked in the hospital section of the nursing home, where the patients needed more care. Some were in bad shape from a broken hip or pneumonia and some patients were in a coma, or too disabled to care for themselves. We would do a bed check every two hours, changing their bedding and turning them over so they wouldn't get bedsores. We also answered their calls. A few patients had a hard time sleeping and others needed medication or liquids throughout the night. Some of the work was hard to do. I would get nauseous if someone threw up or if the men had snotty beds. All in all, the job was good and I also enjoyed the people I worked with.

One night I was sent to check rooms on another floor. I saw this lady in a room by herself and I wondered why she was alone because most of the rooms had two beds. I went in and stood at the foot of her bed for a minute, she seemed so still and quiet. I was just standing there saying a prayer for her and all of a sudden she took a deep breath and she was gone. I had no idea she was so close to death. I stood there for another few moments and said another prayer, and then I went to get the nurses. That was my first experience with someone dying in front of me and I was shook up for a while. Then a nurse told me I would get used to it. I was upset because she said it was something you got "used to." I was also sad that the patient had to die alone.

One morning in February, we had a horrible snowstorm. The day-shift girls couldn't get in and we couldn't get home, so we had to work a double shift. By the time three in the afternoon came around, we were all slaphappy. We got so silly, and laughed so hard we almost peed our pants. We were very tired. Most of the patients couldn't figure out why we were "happy," so to speak. All of us who worked in that department liked our jobs and the patients. There was one sweet, little old lady in her nineties that didn't speak. If you asked her to sing a song, she would break into singing "Take Me Out to the Ballgame" with the sweetest voice. But otherwise she never spoke a word. Everyone loved her; she was such a joy.

Chapter 11

I finally told Stover that *I* wanted a divorce, and this time I was going to make it happen. I was always taught that you couldn't divorce without permission from the bishop if you were married in the church. I went to Father Ott, and he sent me to talk to Father Don. Father Don was in charge of trying to counsel you to see if they could save the marriage or to help you move on. I had told him that I really didn't want a divorce. I wanted Stover to go get some counseling. After months of talking and meeting with me, he then met with the bishop. The bishop finally gave me permission to move forward with a civil divorce.

Father Don also talked to Stover. He flat out told him to let me have what I wanted because he did not care. I told them how Stover beat on me all the time. I also told them how mean he was to our children. Stover just told them, "She never had any bruises on her that would show." I was shocked he would say that to them.

When I got the permission papers, I went to a lawyer and discussed what I should do. He told me I needed to get Stover to move out so we could proceed with the divorce. The lawyer also said I should be able to keep the house, since I still had four kids living at home. Stover, of course, told his mom that I got an annulment, which made her angry at me, but it wasn't true. All I did was get permission from the church to get a divorce, not an annulment.

Stover would not move out, and it was a constant struggle dealing with him all the time. A couple of months later, I decided I had had enough. We were sitting around one evening and I was having a few beers with Ted. Stover was standing in the kitchen doorway and something he said made me mad. I slammed a bottle of beer down on the end table and it put a hole in the table. Then I just threw the bottle at Stover. I missed my target. I guess I should have been glad, because he could have been hurt. I never wanted to hurt anyone and that's why I always kept the peace, until now. A few days later he packed up his things and left, and moved in with his mom. After that he never gave me another dime for the kids.

I went back to the lawyer, and we got started with the divorce. It did not go well. Stover told the judge I was having an affair with a priest. He also told the judge that I wanted my girls to go to a Catholic high school, and he had no intention of paying for it. Stover also said he did not want me to have the house, because he wanted to sell it and pay off our bills, all three thousand dollars we had incurred in debt up to that point.

I couldn't believe all the things Stover told the judge. If I had wanted to have an affair, it would have been with a "man," not a "priest." I had no interest in any man. I felt that sex was horrible, something that you had to do because you were married.

I had many friends who were priest. Father Ott, Father Tom, Father Greg, Father Don, and Father Steve were all close friends of mine. They were my support group, and they were good to me. I never had to fear that they would ever hit me or disrespect me.

Every time I had to go to court, I would end up crying my eyes out over what Stover was doing to us. I was always so upset and in tears that I couldn't speak up for myself. I couldn't fight for myself the way I thought I was prepared to do. When I got before the judge, everything that the lawyer had told me was going to happen didn't happen. It all dissolved before me. The judge kept ruling in favor of Stover and against me.

While all this was going on, I had to get the kids ready for school, and the kids needed shoes. I took them shopping to get shoes, thinking I could use my credit card. After the kids had spent two hours choosing what they wanted, I went to pay. It was then that they told me my husband had my name taken off the credit card, and I wasn't allowed to use it anymore. Stover didn't have the nerve to tell me that he had me taken off the credit card. I thought I could use the credit card until the divorce was final. Kenny got very upset—he needed new shoes the most—but he was afraid to say anything to his dad. He'd learned to steer clear of him a long time ago.

Stover had the nerve to say I was the one who ran the credit cards up. He forgot how many tires he had charged, along with other things he needed for his car. I was only trying to get shoes for our kids for school.

He once had a fit when I bought myself a heavy sweater that cost $25. I paid for it out of my own money—I never charged it to him. His mom was also mad because I paid "so much" for a sweater for myself. With all the stress I was under, I had gained weight, and I needed something to wear that fit. I couldn't afford a new coat, and the sweater seemed like a cheaper alternative. It was the only thing I wore for winter for several years. I couldn't win.

Stover would pick the kids up once in a while on Sundays and take them to his mom's. Most of the time when he brought them home the girls were very upset. They told me that Grandma had pushed their Dad to take everything, including the house away from me and to leave me penniless. The girls could not understand why Grandma would do this to them or to me. They loved her, and so did I. These were her only flesh-and-blood grandchildren. I never ever thought she would be that cruel. What she didn't realize was that she was hurting her grandchildren more that she was hurting me. I could have cared less what she thought of me.

It was a constant struggle with the court. Nothing I said mattered; they would not listen. Stover's aunt had gotten one of the criminal lawyers she worked with to defend him. They were the kind of lawyers who paid judges off to make the right decisions for their client. My lawyer was not fighting for me like he should have. He just stayed silent. I went to another lawyer, and he said something was wrong here. I should get to keep the house since I had four children at home. I told him Stover had told the bank I could not afford the payments, and he wanted the house to be sold. The lawyer agreed to try to help. He spoke to the judge and the other lawyers and he found that there was nothing he could do. Stover was not going to change lawyers.

Stover's mom was very adamant about him taking the house from us. I was in tears all the time, running to church asking for help from the Lord. I would talk to Father Ott, and he could not understand how Stover and his mom could be so mean. Stover's stepdad, Jim, was not involved in any of this. He felt bad for us, but his hands were tied. Dot was running the show. He was always screaming at Dot to leave me be, but there was nothing he could do.

I thanked God that there was at least one person in Stover's family who cared for us and felt bad for us. Jim knew Stover well enough to see through his lies, unlike his mom. She always believed everything he said.

I was up a creek and I knew I was going to lose the house. My son Kenny got mad at me one day and told me that if I "let Dad" take the house, he would never speak to me again. But there was nothing I could do to keep the house.

Kenny was hot tempered and he was missing a lot of school. He had a girl friend that he spent a lot of time with and he didn't want to move away from her. He was very bossy to me, sometimes just like his dad. It got worse after the incident with the "Ginseng seeds." I came home from work one night and Kenny told me the girls weren't in their bed. He said that they had snuck out of the house, but it wasn't true, the girls were in their bed. Then he started crawling around on the floor trying to pick up bugs that weren't there. I realized that something was wrong with him. I called the Life Squad and they took him to the hospital. He was hallucinating on Ginseng seeds that grew in the wild and they pumped his stomach. He was out of control and I didn't know what to do with him.

One day a friend of mine who worked in real estate heard what Stover was selling our house for. She came to me and told me that she could get me a better price for the house sight unseen. She knew it was worth more than what Stover was selling it for. I signed papers to sell the house for the better price but the judge would have no part of it. Stover already had a buyer, who was related to the bank manager, and the judge insisted that the house would be sold to Stover's buyer. He didn't care that I could get more money for it and they just wanted me out of the house. I was sick and tired of crying and fighting and trying to keep the kids happy. It was over. There was nothing else I could do. His family had the money, and they had the upper hand. I may have had no money, no help but I had my children, a job, and my friends. When it came time to settle everything, Stover told the judge he didn't have a job and the judge believed him. He still had the same job that he always had. So the judge ordered him to pay me ten dollars a week for the four kids, I still had at home. Ronnie had joined the navy after he graduated from high school.

Stover sold the house for $21,000 instead of the $24,000 that I was offered. (We paid $14,900 for it twelve years before.) We went to the bank and signed the house away and made everything official. After paying off the remaining bills, we had $6,000 to split. As we were walking out of the bank, Mr. Stover said to me, "Now let's put our money together and buy a new house, and we can get back together." (*Who was the nutty one here?*) I looked at him like he was crazy and said, "After everything you put me through these last few months, not to mention what you've done to the kids and me over the past twenty-three-and-a-half years, you are totally nuts if you think I would ever consider taking you back into our home." I did not want him being mean to my children anymore. I may not have been brave enough to know how to protect them back then, but I did now. After all, the kids had already said, "Mom, we don't need him."

Chris, Barbara, Dorothy and I took our share of the money and tried to figure out where we could live and what we could afford. We had a lot to do. We had to find someplace to live, pack up all of our things and get out of the house on time. We had a deadline, and it was almost Christmas. I could have afforded the house—the payments were only $100 a month but Stover's mom wanted me be destitute, without a home, so I would come back to her son. I wasn't happy about getting a divorce but I felt I had no choice because Stover would not go to counseling.

The feeling of peace I got when everything was over was fantastic; it felt wonderful to be free for the very first time in my life. There would be no more unexpected beatings, no more being screamed at for nothing, and no more being called filthy names. There was also no one putting me down and trying to destroy my self-esteem. Now I had to keep my faith, pick myself up, and move on for my children and myself. After forty years, I was free from abuse. I never wanted to be in that position ever again, and I never ever wanted another man. I was broke, but I was happy.

About a year later, my oldest son, Ronnie called and told me he was getting married. I did not know until the last minute, because his grandma did not want me to know. He eventually told me the morning of the ceremony, and we showed up at the church. Chris and the girls decorated Ronnie's car before we went into the church. We took pictures and took them out to eat afterward. Later, Ronnie's great-aunt Marie, who hardly ever gave them the time of day, gave them a little wedding party, which was very nice for them. They never even invited his sisters and brothers, who would have loved to go. It was their loss. Grandma was not even at the church. She always controlled everything but only came to an occasion when it was convenient for her. Everyone had to go to her. And she always wanted everyone to come see her at her home.

Between working a long twelve-hour night shift at Lakeside Place, cleaning the church, and taking care of the kids, I was very busy but I was happy. There was no crying or fighting and struggling for peace in our home. By this time, Dorothy was in Campbell County High School, and Father Ott talked to me one day about sending Dorothy and eventually Barbara to the parochial school in the area. I knew it would be better for the girls than the public school, but I couldn't afford it. Father Ott said he would see that I got help since I did a lot of volunteer work for the church.

I was doing more and more work around the church. It seemed every time Father complained about not getting enough help around the church, I would take care of what he wanted done so he would quit complaining. One time he was carrying on about not being able to find some church group to scrub down the thirty-foot walls in church. I decided to try to clean the walls myself and I had someone bring me a tall ladder. A few people saw me up on the ladder cleaning the walls and teased me about it. I didn't care; I knew I could do almost anything because I was a hard worker.

I was up and down that ladder a couple of days a week for several weeks. It was hard work but I could see that it was coming clean. One day, when I was almost done scrubbing the walls, the ladder started sliding away from the wall. I was up thirty feet high on the ladder, and I started to cry. I knew it wouldn't do any good to scream, because no one would hear me. I thought I was going to crash into the benches below and get hurt. The ladder kept sliding in slow motion, and all of a sudden it stopped, just that fast. The benches had actually stopped the ladder. I forgot I was in an aisle. I got down and just sat there crying. There was a man who had come into the church just then and saw me crying. But he never said a word.

That was scarier than my worst nightmare. I sat there for a long time and prayed; *thank you God, thank you God, thank you God,* and then I got right back up on that ladder and finished the walls. They looked great. After I was done, I realized how stupid I was, getting on that tall of a ladder and doing the job alone. But Father Ott did appreciate what I had done.

The following school year, Father Ott kept his promise and got me the help I needed to send the girls to the catholic high school. Chris was still in the same grade school.

Around this time I quit working at Lakeside Place and found me a job at Carmel Manor Nursing Home in Fort Thomas. I worked second shift from three to eleven, which was great hours and a much easier job. At this job I made sure all the residents, as they were called and the priest who resided there, had fresh water and whatever else they needed. Then I saw to it that they all made it down to supper. After supper, we made sure the residents had their baths and got them ready for bed. After getting the residents all settled for the night, I would go to the priest side of the nursing home and check on them to make sure they were okay. After that, I could relax until it was time to go home at eleven o'clock. Sometimes we would sit around and chat with the nun who was our supervisor until the end of our shift. It was a much easier job at Carmel Manor, and I really enjoyed the section that I worked in. The residents were not real sick; they just needed to be checked on to make sure that they were all okay.

Sometimes when I would go to talk to Father Ott, and Chris, Dorothy, and Barbara would wait in the car for me. They complained and said that they sat in the car forever. I guess to them it was a very long time and they wanted to get home, but I was having a very difficult time, and I needed someone to talk to besides children.

By this time we were living in a mobile home. We found a pretty nice one that was only three years old, and it was in Claryville, a couple miles past Alexandria. It was only two bedrooms, but we made it work. As long as the kids were happy, so was I. Kenny didn't move into the mobile home with us because he decided to join the marines.

We liked it there until the very first snowstorm in January of 1978 rolled in. It was a blizzard, and we were not able to go anywhere. Everyone was snowed in. After the storm was over, I found someone to move the mobile home to a different mobile-home park in Alexandria. It cost me fifty dollars to have it moved, but it was well worth it. Now I could catch a bus to work and we could walk to nearby stores if we needed to. We were happy. As soon as Grandma heard we moved the mobile home, she made the comment, "Is your mom going to keep moving you around like a bunch of gypsies?" I guess she was still bitter.

Suddenly, Kenny was getting married at seventeen. It was a big hassle. He gave me some money and told me to put something together. I got a luncheon together, and they came to my place after the ceremony to celebrate. Soon after that I became a grandma at the age of forty on January 31, 1978. I went to the hospital to see my beautiful granddaughter named Christie. A few months later in May, my eldest son Ronnie and his wife, had a beautiful baby girl named Kelly, and I was a grandma again. Ronnie and Sharon went on to have three more beautiful children, Lisa, Kevin, and Jamie.

I loved being a grandma, but it was a little sad because we rarely saw the first grandchild, Christie. By this time, Kenny was out of the service—they said he had been too young in the first place, and he and his wife were divorced. Sometimes I would see Christie and her grandma in a store and I would talk to her. I was not allowed to tell her I was her grandma but I could talk to her. That was okay with me at least I got to see her. I did not want to upset her life. Kenny and his ex-wife constantly battled over custody issues with Christie. But her family had money and clout on their side and won out. It was a sad time for Kenny and all of us after that.

Dorothy had graduated from high school and was dating a guy named Earnie. Earnie was spending a lot of time at our house and Ted was hanging around too.

One day while I was ironing, I was talking to Barbara about getting ready for school to start in the fall. It was Barbara's senior year, and Chris was going to be a freshman at Campbell County High School. We were discussing how much money I would need to buy school clothes for them.

Barbara said she wasn't going back to school, and that she wanted to help out with what Chris needed. Barbara was working part-time and had her own money. I told her I wanted her to finish her senior year. It was then that she told me she didn't want to go back to school. I sat down for a few minutes to think, and then said, "Okay, that's fine." Barbara then said she wanted to get married and I said, "To whom?" She went on to say she wanted to marry Ted. I didn't realize that she and Ted were seeing that much of each other because I was working all the time, and the kids never told. I told her we'd figure this out and see what we could do.

I could tell the way Barbara talked about Ted that she loved him; I could see it in her eyes. Ted was a very hard worker and a go-getter, and I could see how much he cared for Barbara. So I agreed to help her the best that I could. Life goes on…

I was just glad I wasn't married to her dad at the time; it could have made things difficult. Stover did like Ted, though, and they were still working together at the same company. So we began planning her wedding. Her dad could not help out because he himself was getting married the next month. So much for Stover's "illness", it was never mentioned again.

We ordered the catering, and her dad did help with some of that cost and we got everything else together. In getting ready for the wedding, we found out that Ted was squeamish around blood. He passed out when they went to get their blood test for the marriage license.

Barbara and Ted had a very beautiful wedding, and I was very happy for them. But the wedding and reception didn't go off without a few kinks. It was the end of October, and it was very hot outside. The inside of the church was also hot, and because of the heat, Ted almost passed out at the altar in the middle of the ceremony. He had to be helped to a chair and sat for a few moments before the wedding could continue.

At the reception, I found out that the bar bill was separate from the cost of the hall rental, and Ted's parents wound up paying it. I felt terrible that I didn't know there would be a separate bar bill and I didn't have the money to pay for it. I had already spent my last dollar on the rental of the hall. I was grateful Ted's parents were able to take care of it.

Barbara and Ted were very happy. The following year they had their first child, a beautiful baby girl named Mary Elizabeth. It was a very happy time and I spent a lot of time with them.

I enjoyed spending time with my family. I would have a birthday dinner for whoever had a birthday that week and sometimes the other kids came to celebrate. I didn't mind, because I enjoyed it when all my kids showed up.

When our mom was sixty-one years old, she had to have open-heart surgery. She insisted that she have the best doctor, and that was Dr. DeBakey. She wanted no one but Dr. DeBakey, and he was in Texas. So that is where she had to go for the surgery. Patty, Shirley, and I flew to Texas together. Three of my children paid for my plane ticket and also gave me some spending money, which was very sweet of them. My older brother Floyd drove from the state of Washington to Texas in his camper with his wife and two youngest kids. It was just great to see him again.

Our mom had her surgery and it went well. After a week she was able to go home. My sisters and I had a good time with my brother while we were in Texas. We wanted to go to Galveston to see the ocean, so we caught a bus and had a great time It was awesome—I loved the ocean. When our mom was able to go home, Patty flew back with our mom and Bill. Shirley and I took a plane home the next day.

It was not long after that when I started getting sharp pains in my right foot. I couldn't walk without pain. I would be cleaning the church and all of a sudden the pain would hit me. Sometimes

I would sit down and cry because it hurt so badly. I went to doctor after doctor and they said they couldn't find anything wrong. I was in a lot of pain, but only when I walked, which seemed strange to me. I had already quit working at the nursing home because of the trouble I was having with my feet. I went to work at the liquor store after the owner of the store, offered me a sit down job. I was also working at the bowling alley and still cleaning the church. I was trying to earn extra money so Chris could go to his prom and also finish high school. The orthothopedic doctors finally decided to do surgery, thinking it was the tendons in my right ankle causing the pain. I was seeing so many doctors.

It was at this time that Mr. Stover offered to help me out by sending some extra money for Chris. He would send me a check and I never questioned him. I was surprised that he wanted to help me after all that he had put me through but I was thankful for the help. I felt that maybe he was trying to make up for some of his past shortcomings. We were always on friendly terms. While I was still on crutches, he even offered to buy me a new dining-room table set. Although I could have used the money for more important things, but it was what he wanted me to have, so I let him.

After I was off the crutches and my ankle was healed, I still had all the same pain in my foot. The surgery did not help. Out of the blue, when Chris was twelve years old, Stover gave me a check for a thousand dollars to take Chris to Disney World. My son Kenny, had been floating between jobs at the time, so Kenny helped to make sure the car was in good shape for the trip.

We asked my nephew Frank Jr. to come along so Chris would have someone his own age to enjoy the trip with. It wasn't much fun for me—I was hobbling around with my cane—but the boys enjoyed the trip. I was so happy for the boys.

When the surgery on my ankle didn't work, they put me in the hospital to see if they could find out what was wrong. One day I heard the doctors coming down the hall, and they were saying, "We just can't find anything wrong with her. It must be in her head." When Ted and Barbara came to visit me, I told them what I heard the doctors say, so Ted said, "Come on, Marian, we are getting you out of here." They took me out the back stairs, and we left the hospital. I eventually went to a foot doctor, and he taped my feet up. After that, I was able to walk without pain, but it didn't last—the doctor couldn't keep my foot taped up forever.

After two years of pain in my feet, I began having pain throughout my whole body. I eventually had to quit working all jobs even the work I did at church that I loved. I had trouble dressing myself and combing my own hair. My hands and fingers were constantly swollen, especially my right hand. My right hand was swollen twice the size of the left hand, and it was very painful. Chris had to help me all the time with putting on my shoes and socks and combing my hair. I couldn't lift my arms up to my head at all. I went to the family doctor, and she figured out that I had arthritis and sent me to a rheumatoid arthritis specialist. I was told I had systemic psoriatic arthritis. I had always had psoriasis pretty bad, but I had never heard of systemic psoriatic arthritis. I found out that *systemic* meant that the inflammation was throughout your whole body, and that psoriatic arthritis is a lifelong condition that causes deterioration of the bones, pain, and stiffness in the joints. She told me to continue to see my family doctor, and she also said she would help me get Social Security because I was so disabled by the psoriatic arthritis, I couldn't work. I was in constant pain and even had to use a wheelchair at times.

It was four years of struggling, trying to make ends meet. Chris was still in high school, and it was hard keeping food in the house for him. I wasn't able to work anymore, and the financial benefits I got from the government, food stamps and a small supplement check, were hardly enough. But we made do. I was able to keep most of the foods that Chris liked to eat, especially his "French fries and catsup". I had been through worse times as a child, but I wanted to do better for my son. I was very lucky that I had lots of good friends. There was one friend in particular,

Beverly, who was able to help me by taking me back and forth to my doctor appointments, and then we would have lunch together. She would also take me with her to her doctor appointments to keep her company. It was good for both of us. We also helped each other by talking on the phone late at night when neither one of us could sleep. One year she even brought me gifts to give to my grandchildren for Christmas. She was such a good friend to me.

After four years, I finally got Social Security benefits, and that helped a lot. We were going to be okay. Chris got a job part-time when he was a senior in high school, at the machine shop where his older brother worked. He wanted to work there ever since Ronnie started working there. He enjoyed the work, and they eventually hired him full-time. They taught Chris and Ronnie different areas of the business.

Barbara and Ted were having another baby and they needed to move out of their small apartment and find something bigger. They bought a really nice mobile home in Crescent Springs, Kentucky, near where we used to rent a house when Barbara was a baby. They were in the same mobile-home park as her Grandma and Grandpa Beahr. Our mom and Bill had previously sold the house in Covington that had belonged to my Grandma and Grandpa Gausepohl and was where our mom was born. They sold the house to my sister Shirley and her husband. On the weekends, Barb and Ted along with their daughter Mary would come to Alexandria—what Ted called "A" town by now—and we would drink quite a few beers and play cards for hours. My sister and her husband would join us too. It was a fun time.

Then Dorothy and Earnie decided to get married, so they went looking for a place to live. Luckily, they found a nice mobile home right up the street from Barbara and Ted and Grandma and Grandpa Beahr. They were excited about their new home, and they really got to know their Grandpa Beahr better. My children really liked being around him, he was a good man.

Grandpa Beahr was a very good influence on my son Kenny. Grandpa and Kenny always rode motorcycles together, and they would take breaks along the way to chat and have lunch. Grandpa Beahr loved his motorcycle. They would ride down to the Red River Gorge in Kentucky. He helped Kenny a lot by giving him fatherly advice and also some good safety riding tips. I appreciated how he helped Kenny, especially with the motorcycle tips, because I worried when Kenny rode his motorcycle. I have always hated motorcycles. Kenny seemed to be a lot calmer after rides with him.

Dorothy and Earnie had a beautiful wedding in September of 1982. She had been saving her money ever since she started working at a company in downtown Cincinnati at the age of eighteen. She knew she wanted a big wedding, and that she would have to pay for it. I felt so bad that I could not help her pay for it. She bought herself a beautiful wedding dress and chose a hat for her headpiece. I put veiling on it for her, and she made a very beautiful bride. She ordered and paid for the cake she wanted, and we did all the catering ourselves. She even paid for the rental of the hall. She was a very hard worker, even working a second job to help pay for the wedding.

I was able to make all the little girls' dresses. She wanted all her nieces to have the same dress, only in different pastel colors. I had forgotten about Nichole, Dorothy's half-sister, who was four years old. I should have made a dress for her too, but she wore a lovely dress that looked similar to the ones my granddaughters were wearing.

Dorothy loved all her nieces and nephews and wanted a picture taken with all of them and her half-sister, Nichole. My grandson Kevin, the youngest, was on her lap, and she let out an "Ouch!" He had bitten her finger because he was teething. We all had a good laugh over that one.

Chapter 12

One Saturday I went to a funeral at another church. During the mass I suddenly got a very uncomfortable feeling; I turned around and noticed that Sister Ina was sitting right behind me. At the time I did not know why I felt uneasy. When I came back from Communion, I moved to another seat in back to get away from her. It was odd the way I felt.

It was then that I started remembering what she had done to me when I was twelve years old in the orphanage. It was such a creepy feeling and I couldn't shake it. I remembered that I had purposely avoided her a few years before this. I tried to stay out of her sight because I knew that she was always hugging everyone, and I did not want to be hugged by her. I had never liked to be hugged by anyone outside my family, and looking back, this was probably why.

Around this time, there was a lot of news about priests molesting children, and it was then that I realized the abuse I received from Sister Ina as a child was called *molestation*. I sat down and wrote a letter to the bishop to let him know that it was not only priests who molested little children—so did the good nuns who were supposedly working for the Lord.

One of the bishop's assistants was asked to call and talk to me about the letter. I knew him because he had been at our parish for a while and we were friends. I was told they wanted me to go to counseling for a while, and I had to tell them exactly what had happened to me. Talking about it was horrible and I cried the whole time. Then they wanted me to confront the nun who had molested me. I thought it was a terrible thing to have to do, but they said you have to confront the abuser if you are going to heal. I don't know if that is true, because I did not feel any better afterward.

When I met to confront her, the first thing she said to me was, "I thought we were friends! I even came to your children's weddings." I told her I thought we were friends too until I remembered what she had done to me as a child. She did not deny the accusation against her. She just sat there quietly after that then finally said, "Can you ever forgive me?"

I was crying the whole time. I did not know how to answer her, so I said, "Maybe someday." I found out during my counseling sessions that there were at least thirteen others who had been molested by the same nun. Soon after, this nun was sent to another parish. The church had a habit of sweeping these things under the rug.

Shortly before my step dad's seventy-fifth birthday, he got really sick. It turned out that he had lung cancer. My daughters decided to throw a birthday party for him. Bill was so happy about the party. Dorothy and Barbara made him a beautiful ceramic stallion, and he also received a motorcycle vase. He cherished them both. The girls loved living close to each other and to their grandparents, especially their Grandpa Beahr. Bill continued to ride his motorcycle that year until he was too sick to ride.

By this time, Mom and Bill had been married for twenty-five years, and we were all very fond of him. He loved when we all came to visit. At first he thought we were coming to see our mom, but he soon came to realize that we were really coming to see him. He enjoyed our company, and we enjoyed his company. He was a wonderful man and we all loved him. He got sicker and sicker, and Mom always had to go out. Bill would sit at the kitchen table and cry. He begged her to stay home with him because he was so sick. He needed her, but she didn't care. She had to go have fun with her friends.

That is when I finally realized why we were in the orphanage. Our mom only cared about herself and no one else.

Barbara tried to help take care of him the best she could. There was only one mobile home in between her grandparents' mobile home and hers, so she was close by and could help. Bill loved seeing her and also spending time with her two kids.

When Bill got worse and went into the hospital, we stayed at the hospital with him. I would spend the night along with our mom, and in the morning, I would run home and get a shower and come back. Our mom always had to leave so she could go bowling because she didn't want to lose her money she had already paid. She wouldn't come back to the hospital until later.

There were several of us in Bill's room one day when he looked up at the crucifix on the wall and said, "I think I am only on the seventh station." He was in so much pain, but he didn't feel like he was ready to go. That was so neat.

The day I thought he was dying, I wasn't going home I wanted to stay with Bill. When I told our mom she said she had to go bowling and that I should go home and get some rest if I was coming back that night. I told Mom I was not leaving, and that we would not be coming back to spend the night because he was dying. She said, "Well, I can't miss my bowling. Call me if you need to." I stayed, and after about four hours she did come back. She told me Barbara said that I called her and told her that Bill was dying. I never called Barbara and told her that. I did tell our mom that Bill was dying before she left to go bowling.

When Bill took his last breath, there were about twelve of his closest family around him. All of a sudden his eyes got real big, and he looked up into the corner of the room like he saw something. It was really quiet, and a calm feeling came across the whole room. We were all in awe; we all felt like he saw something. It was a beautiful experience. He was a wonderful dad and grandpa. We felt like we just lost the only person who ever really cared for us.

Bill passed away the day before our mom's birthday. On her birthday, we were taking her out to eat, and she said to the waitress, "Today is my birthday, and my husband just died, and the kids are taking me out to celebrate." We all just looked at each other and hoped she did not realize what she had just said. That was Rita, our mom.

The day of the funeral, our mom was also acting strange. In church during the Mass, after Communion, our mom got up from the front pew where she was sitting and sat in the very last pew in the church. We were all very puzzled. We guessed she wanted the attention that Bill was getting, and no one went to check on her.

Shortly after Grandpa Beahr passed away, my daughter Dorothy found out she was pregnant with her first baby. She felt bad that she did not get to let him know that she was having a baby. He would have been very happy for her.

Eventually, Kenny started dating Debbie, who had an eighteen-month-old son named Tony. Tony was adorable, and I considered him my grandson. Kenny and Debbie went on to have a daughter they named Angela Dawn, who was also adorable.

Soon after, Dorothy and Earnie had their first child, a beautiful little boy named Jason Reed, and he was absolutely the most adorable little toddler I had ever seen. Jason was such a funny and comical child. I was lucky enough to be able to look after him once in a while for her.

Eventually, my daughters left Crescent Springs and moved closer to me, as did my son Ronnie. I was much happier that they were closer and I was able to see them more often.

Back when Mary was born, I had started what I called "my little black book," and when she and Teddy or any one of the grandkids would say something interesting, I would write it in my book. Jason would say so many neat things that my book was getting pretty full. He was always silly and kept everyone laughing. He was such a happy child.

Kenny and Debbie had a third child, an adorable little boy named Allen. Allen had a big problem, though: he was born with a hole in his heart. I was so worried about him. He was so tiny and could hardly breathe. You could barely hear him cry because he was so weak. I asked Kenny and Debbie if I could take him home from the hospital, mostly because they were moving and I wanted to help with Allen. I watched after him and made sure I took him to see them often while they were moving.

Over the next few months, I cared for him whenever Kenny and Debbie needed a sitter. Several times I took Allen to the hospital during the night because of problems with his medication or his breathing. He was always so grey. It was hard to take him outside—you had to cover his face with a small blanket so he could breathe. I loved caring for him. He was so tiny, and I could still handle him even with my arthritis.

When he was six months old, they finally decided to do open heart surgery to fix the hole in his tiny heart. He was growing weak and not getting enough oxygen. I stayed with him at the hospital the whole time, going home to shower and coming right back. At first, you were not allowed to touch him after the surgery. They wanted him to be very still and not have any excitement so he could heal faster.

When Allen was eight months old, after the surgery, I took him to the pediatrician, and I asked if there was something wrong with him because he did not try to roll over or anything. At first they said he was okay, and then after looking at his chart they decided they needed to do some testing on him. It was then that they figured out that Allen had something called Miller-Dieker syndrome. I had never heard of it, and neither had some of the other doctors. He was going to have serious developmental problems. We had to start taking him for therapy at least once a week. Most of the time I took him by myself, because his mom had her hands full with the other two children at home. I didn't mind at all; I loved Allen and was glad to do it. I loved all my grandchildren.

It was during these times when I was taking Allen to therapy that Barbara announced that she was pregnant with her third child. A few months later the doctors discovered a problem with the pregnancy and they told us that the baby might not make it. We hoped and prayed that they were wrong. When she was seven months pregnant she went to the doctor for an ultrasound and they didn't find a heartbeat. It was the saddest thing I ever had to deal with. It hurt so very badly, and I could not stop crying. Hours later, the baby was delivered and Barbara and Ted named her Melissa Ann.

After everything settled down that evening, I talked to one of the nurses and asked if I was allowed to at least hold the baby. It took a while, but they brought her to me. I had to sit in a certain room to hold her, and they had guards outside the door. She was all wrapped up in a blanket. I held her and rocked her and it was soothing to me. She looked like her big sister Mary, and she was beautiful. My beautiful granddaughter Melissa was gone. My daughter was so upset she couldn't even talk; she and Ted were at least able to hold on to each other. To me this was the most awful thing ever to happen to our family. We later found out that Melissa had something called cystic hygroma that would have required numerous surgeries and still no promises.

Several months later, Barbara read an article in a magazine about cystic hygroma, and she stated that she felt a little better knowing that Melissa did not have to suffer through all the surgeries that she would have had to endure to have a chance at life. Barbara did not want her child to have to go through all that pain. It was a very difficult situation for my daughter and her husband.

This is a poem I wrote for our family.

Mommy carried me ever so carefully
I became weak - I couldn't hang on
I am not gone
I am with Jesus
I remain always in your hearts
I know how much I am loved
My Grandpa Beahr has told me so -
All about my wonderful Mom and Dad.
My Brother and Sister - Mary and Teddy
My Grandparents - Aunts and Uncles.
He will help me help you
Through Jesus - who alone knows our pain
He loves and cares so much
Though there are times, I know
That it doesn't seem so
But he does love us very much,
So much, we can never realize.
I love you Mom and Dad
Mary and Teddy.

Love Melissa Ann

Chris was my last child to get married. Lori and Chris, along with her mother, planned a beautiful wedding. I was asked to make the bridesmaids' dresses because Lori wanted a certain color and style. She chose a beautiful cotton-candy-pink material that was so easy to work with. My hands were still bad with arthritis, but if I took my time, I could do it. The dresses turned out beautifully, and they all fit perfectly.

Lori wanted a veil that was wavy around the edges. I figured out how to do it with fishing wire, and it turned out great. She loved it. I made three of my granddaughters' dresses also, and I even altered the sleeves on Lori's wedding dress. She did not want long sleeves in May, so that was an easy fix.

After all that was done, I had to find myself a dress. I couldn't find anything to wear, so I decided I had to make myself a dress. That was not easy, because I had gotten pretty heavy from all the medication I was on.

The night before the wedding, on our way to the rehearsal dinner, Dorothy and I were almost involved in a car wreck. Luckily, Dorothy pulled to the side when she saw a truck coming up behind her too fast. That truck plowed into the trunk of the car in front of us. We were really shaken up by this. After the scare was over, Dorothy told me that she was pregnant with her second baby, but I wasn't allowed to tell anyone, until she was ready to share the news. I was so happy for her.

On the day of the wedding, everyone needed my help. I was asked to go to the store and also to baby-sit. I was still trying to finish my dress. Help! I was especially ready to scream when another grandchild was dropped off to me. She needed a dress and shoes to wear. My son didn't have time to get them, because he had to be at the church early since he was in the wedding. I ended up having to hot-glue some parts of my dress to make it presentable. I had to get myself ready and also stop at the store to buy some clothes for my granddaughter. Eventually, as usual, I made it.

Our friend Father Ott even assisted at the Mass. He was happy to be there for Chris. It was a beautiful wedding.

Over the years I was allowed back at Dots on weekends and special occasions, for the kids' sake. We were on friendly terms after Stover remarried and I had always remained friends with Stover. I even started to run Dot around again. I never held a grudge, and she was okay.

Not long after Chris's wedding, the children's Grandpa Kiger, (Jim) became ill with leukemia. I often went with my children to visit their grandparents. One evening we were all there, Stover and his wife, our kids and some of Jims' family. Jim was in a lot of pain and he suddenly jumped up out of his chair and yelled to his wife, "Goddamn it, Dot, call Dobbling Funeral Home and tell them to come and get me." The next day, I was with Allen at his therapy when I got a call from one of the kids saying that Jim was in the hospital and he was dying. By the time I got over to the hospital, it was too late. He was already gone. I was very upset because I loved my father-in-law very much, and he had been ill for such a short time.

Soon after Jim passed away, I decided to find out about an annulment. I was thinking that I would feel a little better about being divorced. I filed all the paperwork for the annulment, and my friend Father Don took care of it. When they sent papers to Stover to be completed, he refused to deal with them. So Father just applied for it for me, and I received the papers in July of 1990.

A couple of weeks after Chris and Lori's wedding, several of my children started talking to me about moving and selling my mobile home because I could not do the upkeep, like cutting the grass, now that I was living there alone. They had their own families now and did not have too much time to help.

It took me a while to decide to move and I found myself a nice apartment in Alexandria. It was perfect, except for having to do laundry across the street, and I was still near my family. Shortly after I moved into my apartment, Dorothy and Earnie had another beautiful baby boy named Eric Michael.

On August 15th, 1990, almost exactly one year after we lost Jim, Mr. Stover died suddenly of a massive heart attack on his way home from work one evening. His nephew Mike had been following him because he knew Stover wasn't feeling well. When Stover pulled off to the side of the road, his nephew was there to call for help. I went with the kids to the hospital to see their father. I felt so sorry for them. He was their father, and they loved him. It seemed like too many people were dying all at once. I felt kind of bad about Stover's death. After all, we were married for over twenty-three years, and he was the father of my children.

I was still caring some for Allen, especially when his parents would go on motorcycle rides in the mountains. Sometimes Barbara would watch Tony and Angela when they went on these rides. After he was about four years old, Allen would sit by my big window and wait for them to come get him. He seemed kind of sad. He just wanted to be home with his brother and sister. Allen was a very smart child, but he could not speak. He would not put anything in his mouth, not even candy, and he always had to be fed. We were lucky he was not attached to a lot of tubes and stuff. It wasn't long after that I wasn't able to keep him as much. My arthritis was still bad, and it was much harder for me to handle him as he grew.

In the meantime, we were having meetings with doctors about Allen. His mom did not want to accept Allen's condition, and even his dad was having a hard time. One thing they told us about Allen was that he would never walk. Debbie decided she would not let that happen. She would take him by the arms and walk him every chance she got. By golly, by the age of seven, he was able to walk some. He was wobbly, but he could walk. He still rolled around on the floor a lot to get around.

Allen was a feisty, happy, lovable, sweet little boy, but he could knock you down in a minute he was so strong. He was very hard to handle, but Mom and Dad could do it. He would sit on the floor and listen to music. Music was his favorite thing, along with watching exercise tapes and train tapes. He also loved watching the movie *Dirty Dancing* because of all the dancing. He really loved to dance in his own way. I still tried to help with Allen by taking him to his doctors, but he was a handful for me the older he got. At age five, he was still in diapers, and he always would be. It was so hard to change him because he would roll all over the place very fast.

Allen also liked to pull hair; especially little girls who had long hair. (His big sister and mother had long hair.) Once he got a good grip, it was hard to pry his fingers away. The little girls learned to stay away from him. Even the dogs learned to hide when they saw Allen coming. They wouldn't go near him for fear he would pull their tail and not let go. He was very fast at getting to whatever he wanted.

A few years later Patty and I flew to the state of Washington to visit my brother Floyd and his family. He had lived and worked in Seattle since he left the navy when he was young. I thought we were going to visit with him and his wife and five kids, but we jumped in his truck and camper. We went with him and his wife and drove across the state. I had no idea we would be camping. The trip was very hard on me because of my arthritis, climbing up and down to get in and out of the truck and camper.

We did have a really nice weeklong vacation with them. It was beautiful everywhere we went. We picked blueberries from the bushes outside our camper in the morning for our breakfast, and then we drove all the way across the state to Mount Rainier. We drove up a winding road as far as we could near the top of Mount Rainier. It seemed like we would never reach the top. We went around and around, and just when we thought we were at the top, there were more roads to climb. It was so beautiful at the top. You could even see some skiers up there that looked like little black dots in the snow in the distance. It was a wonderful trip, and it was the best visit with my brother. What a beautiful world the Lord has made for us.

Right after that, our dad passed away at the age of 76, all alone in his apartment. He was found sitting up on the side of his bed, and they said it looked as if he were trying to turn the fan on. We were told he died of heat exhaustion, as the air conditioner in the building was malfunctioning. Our dad came back to live in the area a few years before and he was living in a building for seniors. My sisters and I had would take him to the store when he had needed groceries. He also wanted to have lunch at the Anchor Grill in Covington because it was his favorite place to eat. We barely knew our dad, but we knew who he was. He always managed to find a phone number and call us once in a while, but we never knew what to say to him because he was a stranger to us.

I asked him once, "Why were we in the orphanage if we still had two parents?" He told me that it was my great-aunt Henrietta's idea; she thought we were too much for our mom and that she could not take care of us. My next question was, "Why couldn't you care for us?" I got no answer. We found out that he had donated his body to science, so they took care of that. Then we went to one of my priest friends, Father Don, and asked if we could at least have a memorial Mass for him. After all, he was our dad. Father had a beautiful service for him. We had nothing to feel guilty about. He was now in the hands of the Lord. Amen.

Chris and Lori were having their first baby. Lori was a nurse, and she was working at the hospital the night she went into labor. They kept Lori there after her shift was over, and sure enough, the baby was born the next morning, an adorable little girl named Megan, and she was beautiful. When Megan six weeks old, Chris asked if I would watch her for them, and I said sure I would. I loved babies, and I told him I would do it as long as I could. I did not know how long I could handle her with the arthritis. I was worried that as she got older, she might be too heavy for me. She never did get too heavy; the more I watched and handled her, the easier it got. My arthritis was easing up, so I was even able to continue watching their next child, a beautiful little boy named Matthew. He was also adorable.

I also helped baby-sit my other grandchildren once in as while. One time I was going somewhere and I had Mary, Teddy and Jason in the car. I was going down this new road and before I knew it the road came to an abrupt end. We went flying across a drop off and the kids hit their heads on the roof of the car. They thought it was funny and they started calling me "Stunt grandma". It wasn't funny to me; I was scared for the kids and I've never lived it down.

I had always remained friends with Father Ott. He had heart problems and had to leave our parish, and eventually he ended up living in the Carmel Manor Nursing Home. I would take him things that he thought he needed, like root beer and even beer for him to give to the nuns. Since my only "job" was babysitting my grandchildren, I had time to help him out. He was a dear friend.

Father Ott always thought he had lots of friends, especially from our parish since he had been there for quite a while. But hardly anyone showed up to visit him except for a few fellow priests. He really wanted to see his friends. It's a lonely life for the elderly in nursing homes, especially for priests who didn't have their own families. Sometimes I would take Megan with me to the nursing home, and all the elderly people would fall all over her. They loved children, but she was a little shy. She was adorable with beautiful long blond hair, and I was very proud of her.

This one particular day I wasn't planning to visit Father, but I knew he was having trouble walking and getting weaker, so I went anyway. When I got there, he asked me to go get him some root beer because he was out. His sister was there when I arrived, but she left after paying his bills. I went to the store and picked up the root beer, and when I came back I sat down to talk with him. The day before, he'd had some problems, and could hardly walk, so I decided to stay and help him down to supper. I was talking with him and would ask him a question, and he would give me an odd answer. He was talking like he was still building the new church at our parish that was already built.

I finally told him to get comfortable in his chair and get some rest, and that I would stay and help him down to supper and he was okay with that. Just after he put his head back to relax, he took his last breath. I couldn't believe it so I went running for the nurse. (I used to work there, but I had forgotten that there were buttons you could push for the nurses.) But he was gone. He passed away on April 16, 1993 a few days after his seventy-sixth birthday. He went very peacefully, and I know he was with his Lord who he loved very dearly. Father Ott was a little different, even odd at times, but he was a very good, faithful, and strict priest.

It was that same year that my brother Floyd had been in the hospital off and on for a few weeks with a lot of back pain. After a few weeks of trying to figure out what was going on with him, they sent him home. He was still in a lot of pain. The next morning, his wife went to work and Floyd stayed home. When his wife got home from work, she found my brother lying on the floor near the bathroom and he was dead. He had passed away at the age of fifty-seven of a massive heart attack on July 22, 1993, just three days after his 57th birthday. Patti called and told me that Floyd had died. I felt like such a big baby because I cried so hard and I could not stop crying. I loved my brother very much and that was the second worst loss I had ever felt. It was hard to believe that death could hurt so much. That night, my brothers, sisters and I all went together to tell our mom. When we told her, she just sat there and said, "I loved him." I hate to say it, but she never shed a tear, at least not while we were there. I felt bad for her then because she was never really close to any one of us.

A few days later, Patty and I flew to Washington, and our sister Beverly flew up from Philadelphia to join us. Patty and I were bad—we scheduled her on a flight that coincided with our mom's flight, so they would have each other to talk to. Later we got hell from Beverly for putting her on the same plane with our mom. We knew she wouldn't like being on the same flight with our mom, because they didn't get along.

My sisters Shirley and Sandy along with my brother Frankie rented two cars and drove to Washington. Shirley's husband, Jim, and their daughter Cindy also came. Our brothers Harry and Ron were flying up later. My sister Gerry could not make it.

We spent three days there and got to visit with all of our nieces and nephews.

Chapter 13

Our mom had been sick off and on for a couple of years and ended up in the hospital a few times. (One time she had gall-bladder surgery and because of some issue with her medication, she ended up losing function in one of her kidneys.) About a year after Floyd died, she went to her family doctor because she was feeling tired. Her family doctor didn't want to do heart surgery on her because she only had one functioning kidney. So she went to a different doctor who would do the surgery.

Patty and I tried to tell her that it was not feasible for her with all her problems. We knew her family doctor had advised her against the surgery. She said, "Other people my age have heart surgery, why can't I? I want to have this surgery because if I can't *dance*, I do not want to live." Patty and I just looked at each other and shook our heads. We didn't know what to think. Our mom didn't want to hear it. She would not listen to anything we had to say.

Our mom went on to have the surgery, and she did not wake up for a few days. When she did, she didn't know any of us. She'd had a stroke in the brainstem area and they said that she might not recover from the surgery. After a few days, the nurses talked to us about taking care of her affairs.

We all knew that my brother Ron was the one she had chosen to be in charge of her affairs. Ron said he did not have the time to take care of everything, because of his work schedule. He knew there was a lot work to be done and he suggested that I look into what needed to be done. So I spoke with a lawyer to find out what we needed to do. The lawyer immediately drew up the papers. A few days later, my brother, sisters and I went to a meeting with the social worker at the hospital to discuss our mom's situation. The social worker told us she needed full-time care, and they suggested a nursing home. None of us were equipped to care for someone in her condition. I knew how hard it would be to care for her, because I had cared for patients in her condition when I worked in the nursing home. Most of us felt the nursing home would be the best choice. The nurse took the papers to our mom and explained the situation to her, and she signed them. To this day, I do not believe she knew what she was signing it was sad.

Later I went to the cafeteria to get a drink with some of my family, and we sat and talked about how awful this was. This was such a serious situation, and it all seemed very sad to me. She had been a very active woman, and she enjoyed her later years doing lots of activities with her friends.

There was so much to do. We had to get our mom signed up for assistance in order for her to go into the nursing home and we had to give up her apartment. We were also told that if she had any money at all, we should take it to the funeral home for her burial arrangements. Then the social worker told us we had to take the first nursing home that was available within a twenty-mile radius.

In moving her belongings out of her apartment, we decided it would be best to take her belongings and keep them at our homes, and if she recovered we would give them back. Her jewelry was kept together in case she wanted some of it at the nursing home. We had to tell our mom that we had to give up her apartment.

This really upset her because she couldn't comprehend what had happened to her. I tried to explain to our mom why this had to be done, and she seemed to understand. We were only doing what the social worker had told us to do. It was all very upsetting and hard to deal with.

While the paperwork was being taken care of our mom was transferred to a nursing home in Indiana. I was running back and forth to Indiana every other day trying to get all the paperwork straightened out, and then I would spend some time visiting with her. Most of the time when Patty was off work, she would go with me. I always went on the days I was not babysitting my two youngest grandchildren. We enjoyed the trip most of the time, always taking time to have lunch and visit the antique shops in Indiana when we finished visiting with our mom. One day during our visit, she told us that she had a boyfriend who was her neighbor across the hall.

On Mother's Day, Patty and I had decided to take our mom out to eat. She was sitting outside when we arrived and she did not know who we were until we told her. We told her we came to take her to breakfast at Frisch's for Mother's Day, and she said, "I would like that". She enjoyed it when she was able to go somewhere.

Once when I took our mom's two sisters, Edith and Marian, to visit her, she thought I was her sister Edith. On Thursday of that same week, my sister Joan and I went to visit with her. While we were there, Joan got into a very loud argument with her. I was not in the room, but I could hear them yelling down the hall. I could not understand why Joan was arguing with her in her condition. Our mom was very upset and did not understand. She told me that she did not know what Joan was talking about and that Joan must be crazy for cussing her out like that for no reason.

After we left, I asked Joan why she was arguing with our mom. Joan told me she asked our mom why she put us in the orphanage and why she did not want any of us. Joan wanted answers, just like we all did, but it was too late. We weren't going to get any answers now, because our mom didn't remember those times. She could not even remember her own age, and it upset her very badly. I don't think Joan realized how bad our mom's condition was. I always thought that our mom just blocked everything out about our childhood and tried to do the best that she could to get through life. It was sad, because she missed so much of our lives growing up.

On Saturday, May the 14th I went to visit our mom, and she was real quiet and seemed very tired. Since I had worked in nursing homes before, I took her pulse. I thought her pulse was racing, so I called her nurse. The nurse checked her pulse and said it was fine. I knew from past experience that it was not good; I had seen it too many times. When I got home that afternoon, I called as many of my brothers and sisters as I could reach and told them that they better go to visit her now because I didn't think she would be here very long.

I couldn't reach my sister Shirley, who was at a bowling tournament, or my brother Harry. I called my sister Beverly in Philly and told her that if she wanted to see our mom alive, she better come now. Beverly was going to fly in, and she was to stay with me. The very next day, the nursing home called and said our mom had passed away around ten o'clock that morning on May the 15th. She was seventy-five years old.

I called as many of my brothers and sisters as possible. I called my daughter who was across the street, visiting her Grandma Dot. (Dot had since moved across the street from me) and Dorothy came over right away. Dorothy, Patty, and I went over to the home right away to see her. While we were there, they asked us if we wanted to pack up her belongings and take them with us. We did that, but we decided to leave some of her clothes there for the other residents who might need them. The nursing home was happy to keep them.

The following day, my brothers and sisters came to my home to choose the dress for our mom to wear and to distribute the jewelry that had belonged to her. We chose our moms favorite dancing dress. I am not a jewelry person, and I didn't want any of it. The others divided up most of the jewelry except for a few rings that she had. We were going to draw names for the rings later, except for her wedding ring from Bill. We wanted to give it to Bill's daughter, because we knew he would have wanted her to have it.

While we were at the funeral home, there was a sudden commotion. A big argument started, and just as quickly as it started, the funeral director stepped in and put a stop to it. I knew everyone was upset and angry, they didn't expect her to pass away so soon. Our mom is now in heaven enjoying the peace of the Lord.

When my son Chris and his wife, Lori, were expecting their third child, they started building a new home. Chris suggested that I move in with them to make it easier on me when I watched their children. At first I didn't want to move in with them. After I thought about it for a while, I figured it really would be easier on me not having to run out in the rain and snow to go to their home to watch the little ones. It was also getting hard for me to drive at night, especially in the rain. Chris finished off the basement of his home and made part of it into a fully equipped "apartment" for me with its own entrance. It was like a house inside of a house. He also included a few handicap-accessible features to help me with my arthritis. It was a lovely and cozy place to live and to be so near to my grandchildren and watching them grow up, was awesome.

Grandma Stover
Thoughtful,
Caring,
Talented,
Wishes to travel to different places,
Dreams of the Life she's Living,
Wants to enjoy her grandchildren and
     greatgrand children.

Who Wanders what crazy ideas my daddy
     Will have next.

Who is afraid of flying in planes.
Who Likes tulips.
Who believes in angels and Heaven.
Who Loves her Family.
Who Loves dogs and animals.
Who plans parties.

Whose final destination is Heaven.
          Megan Stover 4c
          January 26, 2001

Written by my lovely granddaughter Megan.

A few days before we were scheduled to move in, my last grandchild, Michelle Ann, was born. She was a beautiful baby and she just happened to be my last grandchild. I moved into the house first so that I could help with the kids while they moved. I loved it; I couldn't wait to help with Michelle and continue to watch Matthew and Megan. They were so easy to watch. I lived with my son and his family for thirteen years and then moved into my own home.

Four months after Michelle was born, my first great-grandchild, Chelsie, was born.

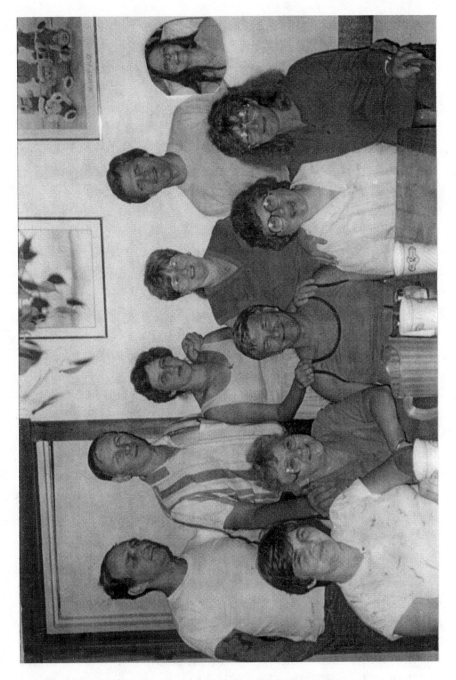

All ten of my brothers and sisters in 1978.

Over the years, my sisters, brothers and I got together for many occasions; weddings, birthdays, funerals, and family reunions. I pretty much always kept in touch with all of them, at least by phone. In 2001, we were planning a Gausepohl Family Reunion. The Monday before the reunion, my sister Joan and I spent the day shopping for yellow t-shirts, which was our family "color" for the reunion. I needed to be home by two o'clock because I was watching my three youngest grandchildren while their parents were on a trip. Joan wanted to stay long enough to say Hi to the kids when they came home from school. She called me later that evening to tell me she got into a fight with a neighbor, and she was laughing about it. Around ten o'clock Joan's daughter Theresa, called to tell me about the fight her mom had with the neighbor. While I was talking to Theresa, I heard Joan hollering that she was having chest pains, so Theresa and her brother, who had been visiting, took her on to the hospital. Around 2:30am, my niece Theresa called and told me Joan had passed away. It was so hard to believe, since I had just spent the day with her. She died at the age of sixty-six from heart disease. This just happened to occur the morning of 9-11.

Staying active with my children and grandchildren over the years has helped to ease the arthritis, and also helped me to become more mobile. I now have sixteen grandchildren and fourteen great-grandchildren, going on fifteen, and I spend my time helping them out when I can. In my spare time, I go on trips with family and friends, play cards, have lunch with nieces and nephews, and go to senior meetings with all my friends. I am enjoying my life.

A few years ago, I went to the Children's Home (formerly an orphanage) to see if they had any records on any of us. They gave me a record for all of us. On the record for the first seven of us who were sent to the orphanage, it said the following under "Habits of Father": "Drinks, will not work steady, and does not seem very interested in the children or their welfare." And under "Habits of Mother," it stated, "Does not like to stay home with her children, becomes frustrated, and does not know how to manage so many children." On the records for the three younger ones who came later to the home, there were no comments entered.

I know from being a mother myself that I could not do what our mom did. I cannot imagine letting someone take my children from me and not even trying to keep them. I also don't understand how she continued to have more children only to also let them be taken away from her. It was not right what our mom did to us, and I will never understand it. The feeling of not being wanted by our parents will be with us forever. Not too long ago, someone asked me if I ever forgave my parents. I thought about it for a while and didn't feel that I needed to forgive them.

Only God knows why our mom allowed this to happen to us. Sometimes I wonder what happened to her in her young life that caused her not to care for her own children. She missed so much of her children's lives. I know now we were better off in the orphanage than living with our parents. We were well taken care of and received a good education. Despite our difficult childhood, we all turned out pretty good.

Many times I have also been asked, "Why did you stay in such an abusive marriage? First of all, I thought our marriage was normal. We did have some happy times but I was scared of him and I was scared to leave him. I grew up in an orphanage and didn't know what went on in the world. I was married at sixteen, and I knew nothing about relationships and what marriage was supposed to be like. After we had children, he always threatened to take them away from me, and I was not going to let that happen. No matter what I had to do to keep, my children they were mine, and I wanted them. I definitely did not want my children to know the feeling of not being wanted. I may not have been the best mother in the world, but I know I did the best I could.

Another reason why I stayed in the marriage was because I was married in the church and was told you didn't get divorced.

It is so hard to understand how I was so thoroughly controlled for the first eighteen years of our marriage Stover kept me to

169

himself and didn't let me socialize with other people other than our immediate families for many years. I was physically, mentally, and verbally abused and controlled. I believed everything he told me. If I even thought something was white, no I was wrong; he would tell me it was black. I was so brainwashed.

To this day, I do not understand how I could have let that happen. Except maybe for the way I grew up in the orphanage—I was used to being told what to do. I was used to being beaten to the ground and then getting up and pretending nothing had happened. I just thought it was normal. It wasn't until my children got into school and I started making friends that I began to realize it was not a normal relationship, and I did not have to live like that.

I often find myself wondering if I am allowing myself to be controlled by others to this day. And then I think no, I just like doing things for others and helping people out. This is just the way I am, and it makes me happy. I thank God that I am physically able to help them as much as I can.

If you have never lived through an abusive situation, it is almost impossible to understand why you would stay. To really understand what physical, mental, verbal, and sexual abuse does to you, you have to have lived through it. You never fully get your self-esteem back. I am lucky to have survived, and I was able to survive it all through the grace of God! I have and always will hold on to my faith and trust in my Lord Jesus.

Amen!

CPSIA information can be obtained at www.ICGtesting.com
Printed in the USA
LVOW092036210512

282662LV00003B/1/P